Canadian Women
NOW + THEN

More than **100** Stories of **Fearless Trailblazers**

Written by **Elizabeth MacLeod**
Illustrated by **Maïa Faddoul**

KIDS CAN PRESS

CONTENTS

Introduction 4

ACTIVISTS

Anjali Katta 6
Viola Desmond 7

ACTORS

Lilly Singh 8
Mary Pickford 9

ARCHITECTS

Brigitte Shim 10
Esther Marjorie Hill 11

ASTRONAUTS

Jennifer Sidey-Gibbons 12
Roberta Bondar 13
Julie Payette 14

CULTURE KEEPERS

Siyamiyateliyot
(Elizabeth Phillips) 16
Shanawdithit 17

DANCERS

Santee Smith
(Tekaronhiáhkhwa) 18
Karen Kain 19

DOCTORS

Samantha Nutt 20
Emily Stowe 21

ENGINEERS

Ayah Bdeir 22
Elsie MacGill 23

ENTREPRENEURS

Melissa Sariffodeen 24
Rose Fortune 25

ENVIRONMENTALISTS

Severn Cullis-Suzuki 26
Anahareo (Gertrude Bernard) 27

EXPLORERS

Susan R. Eaton 28
Charlotte Small 29

FILMMAKERS

Deepa Mehta 30
Judith Crawley 31
Sarah Polley 32

INVENTORS

Hayley Todesco 34
Susan Olivia Poole 35

JOURNALISTS

Sook-Yin Lee 36
Mary Ann Shadd 37

LAWYERS

Denise Dwyer......................... 38
Violet King Henry 39

MATHEMATICIANS

Karen Yeats 40
Cecilia Krieger 41

MILITARY MEMBERS

Jennie Carignan 42
Michelle Douglas 43

MUSICIANS

Tegan and Sara 44
Portia White 45

OLYMPIANS

Penny Oleksiak 46
Fanny "Bobbie" Rosenfeld 47
Clara Hughes 48

PAINTERS

Christi Belcourt 50
Emily Carr 51

PARALYMPIANS

Aurélie Rivard 52
Chantal Petitclerc 53

POETS

Rupi Kaur 54
Pauline Johnson
(Tekahionwake) 55

POLITICIANS

Julie Lemieux 56
The Famous Five 57

SCIENTISTS

Nivatha Balendra 58
Harriet Brooks Pitcher 59

WRITERS

Dionne Brand 60
L. M. Montgomery 61
Margaret Atwood 62

Follow in Her Footsteps 64

More Inspiring Canadian Women 66

Important Dates in Canadian Women's
History 76

Resources 78

Index 79

Canadian Women Are Amazing

THEN+NOW

CANADIAN WOMEN HAVE ALWAYS BEEN GROUNDBREAKERS.
They have fought discrimination, made scientific discoveries, set sports records and much more.

Breaking new ground isn't easy. Many of the people in this book had to battle incredible odds to follow their dreams. In the late 1800s, when Canada was still a new country, most women were told that their only place was in the home. They were discouraged from attending university ("too strenuous!") or playing sports ("too inappropriate!"). A lot has changed since then.

Throughout this book, you'll meet individuals from the present and the past. Those in the NOW category are doing inspirational work in their fields today. Beside them, in the THEN category, are the groundbreakers from the past who paved the way. And some women were groundbreakers in one career and *continue* to inspire today in a different area — you'll find them on the THEN + NOW pages.

You'll meet Indigenous women, some born before the country was founded, whose ancestors were the First Peoples on the land. You'll also read about immigrants who have helped shape the country. Together, they make up the story of Canada.

It's impossible to fit every amazing Canadian woman into one book. But on these pages, you'll discover stories about well-known individuals and even a few you may not have heard about yet. Get ready to meet these remarkable people!

NOW

> *If we give a girl a chance … imagine how different the world would be.*

Anjali Katta

Born: 1997
Birthplace: Sudbury, Ontario

Since the age of six, Anjali Katta has been helping people. She's made jewellery to raise money for the British Columbia Children's Hospital, helped in soup kitchens and volunteered with groups in India, where her parents were born.

One day, while visiting Mumbai, India, Anjali met girls her age who were forced to work instead of getting an education. Some were forbidden to go to school because their parents were worried the boys there would harass them. To help girls like them, Anjali founded GirlsCo. when she was 16 years old. The not-for-profit organization raises money for girls' education.

One of the organization's projects is Bombay Pads. It delivers menstrual products and sex education to girls and women in Mumbai so that girls don't have to miss school or be shamed for not having such products. That means they have a better chance of keeping up with their classmates.

In 2014, Anjali spoke to the United Nations on the International Day of the Girl. She talked about what it means to be a girl and how, in some parts of the world, girls are made to feel unimportant. But, she said, girls are actually capable and strong.

A year later, Canada's government set up the Girls Advisory Council to find out what is important to Canadian girls. Anjali was chosen to advise the council. She wants to empower girls in Canada and raise awareness about the difficulties that girls face around the world.

GirlsCo. also holds conferences across the country to encourage young people to become activists, just like Anjali.

Viola Desmond

1914–1965

Birthplace: Halifax, Nova Scotia

THEN

When Viola Desmond's car broke down in New Glasgow, Nova Scotia, in November 1946, she had no idea she was about to make history. Stuck there overnight, this quiet hairdresser decided to see a movie.

Viola bought her ticket and found a seat on the main floor. But her ticket was for the balcony — only white people could sit in the theatre's better section. Black people, like Viola, had to sit upstairs. An usher told Viola to move, so she tried to buy one of the more expensive tickets for the main floor. The ticket seller refused. This was the last straw. Viola had put up with racism all her life. She slapped down her money and returned to her original seat. Eventually, a police officer took her to jail.

Viola was charged with cheating the Province of Nova Scotia. She hadn't paid the extra one-cent tax for her seat on the main floor of the theatre. No one mentioned Viola's skin colour, but everyone knew that's what the case was really about. She was found guilty and had to pay a fine. Viola fought her conviction but lost. Black people were still discriminated against.

Her story might have ended there, if not for another strong woman — Viola's sister. Many years after Viola died, Wanda Robson began telling her sister's story. People agreed Viola had been treated unfairly. In 2010, Nova Scotia's premier apologized to Viola and all the province's black people and granted Viola an official pardon. Viola Desmond now appears on the 10 dollar bill, making her the first black woman on a Canadian banknote.

Wonderful Women!

Journalist **Carrie Best** *(1903–2001) made Viola's story front-page news to publicize the discrimination she faced. Carrie's newspaper,* The Clarion, *was the first in Nova Scotia owned and published by a black person.*

7

NOW

Lilly Singh

Born: 1988
Birthplace: Scarborough, Ontario

"Whaddup! It's your girrrl, Superwoman!"

If you've ever watched Lilly Singh's videos, then you know that's how they begin. And you probably have — her videos have been viewed about 3 billion times! She's become one of YouTube's biggest stars.

Lilly comes across as confident, but she wasn't always that way. After studying psychology in university, she didn't know what she wanted to do. She began making YouTube videos in 2010 to cope with depression. Lilly decided to use the name IISuperwomanII for her channel. That's because when she was a kid, she believed she had an invisible *S* on her chest like a superhero. It made her think she could do anything.

Lilly writes, directs and stars in her videos. They often show her Punjabi culture, and she plays characters based on her mom and dad. Her fans (Lilly calls them "Team Super") love watching her make comedy out of everyday life. Lilly has also appeared in movies and has several of her own web series.

As well as being an actor, Lilly is a comedian, singer and music video producer. She is also a social activist. In 2016, she began her campaign #GirlLove to encourage positivity and support among girls and women. Lilly spread the message by having celebrities talk about why it's cool for women to help one another. She also works with the organization ME to WE to raise money for girls' education in developing countries.

Lilly created the word *bawse* (rhymes with *house*) to describe someone who is confident and a boss at life. She encourages every girl and woman to be a bawse! In 2019, Lilly became the host of her own late-night talk show.

Mary Pickford

1892–1979

Birthplace: Toronto, Ontario

Gladys Louise Smith didn't want to act in films — she thought they weren't as good as live theatre. But she was tired of making so little money for her roles. So in 1909, when she had a chance to act in a film and earn better pay, she changed her mind about movies. She also changed her name to Mary Pickford.

On Mary's first day of filming, she earned five dollars and was asked to return the next day. She said she would, but only if she was given ten dollars! Mary got the raise and began to like acting in films.

Moviegoers loved the spunky characters that Mary played. By now, she was living in Hollywood and became known as "America's sweetheart." Mary wasn't afraid to ask for more money for her work. Filmmakers thought she was rude for demanding higher pay, but she was one of film's most popular stars and expected her pay to show it. In the early 1900s, when most women didn't work outside the home, Mary earned up to $350,000 per movie. At age 24, she was Hollywood's first millionaire.

It wasn't long before movie studios couldn't afford Mary's salary. She also wanted more control over the kinds of movies she made. So in 1919, Mary became a cofounder of United Artists studio along with three men in Hollywood, including Charlie Chaplin. Soon she was starring in, producing and distributing her own movies. No woman had done this before.

Mary won two Academy Awards, one in 1930 for the film *Coquette* and a lifetime achievement award in 1976. But more important, she paved the way for independent women in Hollywood.

NOW

Brigitte Shim

Born: 1958
Birthplace: Kingston, Jamaica

Born in Jamaica to Chinese parents, Brigitte Shim arrived in Toronto with her family as a child. It was winter, and she felt she had stepped into a gigantic freezer! A few days later, she got her first glimpse of snow when a blizzard hit. Being surrounded by snowflakes made Brigitte appreciate Canada's natural beauty — an experience that would influence her as an architect.

While studying architecture at the University of Waterloo, Brigitte met her husband, Howard Sutcliffe. They formed their own firm in 1994, Shim-Sutcliffe Architects based in Toronto. The company quickly became famous for its creative and sophisticated designs. They have won many prestigious awards, including 14 Governor General's Medals in Architecture! It's important to Brigitte that her buildings fit into their surroundings and incorporate local traditions, materials and construction techniques.

One of Brigitte's most famous designs is for her own home, Laneway House in Toronto. Many architects might choose expensive materials for their homes. But for Laneway House, Brigitte combined inexpensive materials, such as concrete, with higher-quality ones, such as mahogany. The house's location was also an unusual choice — it's in a laneway between the neighbours' garages! Brigitte hopes that her home will show how laneways can be a better use of space for cities.

Another of Brigitte's world-famous designs is Weathering Steel House in Toronto. Even rock star David Bowie asked to take a tour inside this unusual home!

Esther Marjorie Hill

1895–1985

Birthplace: Guelph, Ontario

It wasn't easy for women to become architects a hundred years ago. Esther Marjorie Hill found that out when studying at the University of Toronto. Her male classmates made rude comments, and her professors ignored her. Esther was determined to succeed and, in 1920, she became the first woman to earn an architecture degree in Canada.

After graduating, Esther applied to the Alberta Association of Architects so she could work in the province. But one examiner didn't approve of female architects. Esther was told she wasn't qualified enough, and her application was denied. She took more courses in Toronto and New York and reapplied to the association in 1925. Finally, she was accepted! She was the first woman to become a registered architect in Canada.

Many architecture firms wouldn't hire Esther because she was a woman. From 1925 to 1928, she found work at a New York company. By 1928, she had become an assistant at an Edmonton firm. Then the Great Depression hit. There was little building — or work for architects. Esther lost her job.

After World War II, there was again money for building. Esther opened a firm in Victoria, British Columbia. With her modern, straightforward style, she designed apartment buildings, churches, houses and retirement homes. But she still battled discrimination. Once, a male client tried to take credit for Esther's designs, claiming she had only drawn up the plans!

Esther became a busy, successful architect, sometimes designing three houses a week! She paved the way for women in her field.

Wonderful Women!

Esther was not the only groundbreaker in her family. Her mother, **Jennie Stork Hill** *(1866–1939), was one of the first women to study at the University of Toronto!*

NOW

Jennifer Sidey-Gibbons

Born: 1988
Birthplace: Calgary, Alberta

When Jennifer Sidey was four years old, she heard Roberta Bondar give a talk about being an astronaut. Roberta had been the first Canadian woman to go into space. From that moment, Jennifer wanted to be a scientist like Roberta and maybe one day explore places beyond our world, too.

Her chance came many years later, in 2016, when the Canadian Space Agency put out a call for astronauts. As an engineer who specialized in the science of flames, Jennifer was well qualified for the job. She became one of the 17 finalists who went through months of interviews and aptitude tests. They had to escape from a capsule in rough waters, plug a hole in a flooding compartment and solve puzzles while holding their breath at the bottom of a pool.

Jennifer had the courage and skill to persevere. On July 1, 2017, she was named one of Canada's astronauts. She soon moved to the NASA facility in Houston, Texas, to begin training for missions to the International Space Station and beyond.

Jennifer is grateful for pioneering women such as Roberta. She, too, wants to be a role model for girls who love science. So Jennifer cofounded a chapter of Robogals, an organization that inspires girls to become interested in engineering and similar fields. She has also taught computer programming to thousands of girls across Great Britain.

One of the things Jennifer likes best about space travel is that it brings together people from around the world. She also loves the possibility of visiting unexplored planets.

Roberta Bondar

Born: 1945
Birthplace: Sault Ste. Marie, Ontario

Model rocket ships cluttered Roberta Bondar's bedroom when she was a kid. She loved reading science fiction and even tried to contact space aliens on her radio. Whenever she heard about a space flight on the news, she imagined herself strapped in with the astronauts. She dreamed of being just like them one day. But there was a big problem — Canada didn't have a space program.

Roberta also loved science. In university, she trained as a neurologist (a doctor who specializes in the nervous system). Then, in 1983, Roberta heard that Canada was putting together its first team of astronauts. She applied immediately. From more than 4000 applicants, Roberta was one of the six chosen! She was Canada's first female astronaut.

Even though Roberta had always wanted to go into space, she turned down her first chance. She was offered a job to study the effects of weightlessness on women aboard Russia's *Mir* space station. But Roberta felt she was invited only because she was a woman, not because she was a skilled scientist. So she said no.

Roberta finally flew into space in January 1992 on the American space shuttle *Discovery*. She spent eight days on board, taking photos and working on experiments to help astronauts stay in space longer. She later led a team at NASA looking at how the human body recovers after being in space.

Roberta's time in space got her thinking about the future of the planet. In 2009, she set up the Roberta Bondar Foundation to educate people about the environment and caring for Earth.

Wonderful Women!

When Roberta was a teenager, her aunt **Erma Herman** *(1921–2018) worked for NASA. She often sent Roberta information about the space program to encourage her niece's interest in space.*

13

THEN+NOW

Julie Payette

Born: 1963
Birthplace: Montreal, Quebec

When I saw the earth from above ... it drove home the fact that there's one place where we can live right now. The seven billion of us are sharing a wonderful planet.

Written on Julie Payette's favourite mug is the saying "Failure is not an option." Even when she was a young girl, Julie was ambitious, curious and determined.

At university, Julie studied electrical engineering. Then, in 1991, she applied to the Canadian Space Agency to become an astronaut. Julie was chosen from more than 5300 applicants. To prepare for space, she learned to fly a plane, took scuba diving lessons and studied Russian so she could speak with the astronauts from Russia's space program.

Julie rocketed into space in 1999 to join a team aboard the International Space Station (ISS). She was the first Canadian to set foot on the space station. Her main job was to operate the Canadarm attached to the ISS. Julie used the robotic arm to move cargo and continue building the space station. From 2000 to 2007, she was the Canadian Space Agency's Chief Astronaut, representing Canadian astronauts and organizing their schedules. In 2009, Julie returned to the ISS once more.

Between her own space missions, Julie worked at the NASA mission control centre in Houston, Texas, as the capsule communicator. When astronauts have problems in space, they call the capsule communicator, stationed on Earth.

Julie retired as an astronaut in 2013. Four years later, she became Canada's Governor General, the fourth woman to hold the job. Julie encourages Canadians to get involved in science. She also hopes to see people work together on important issues such as climate change, Indigenous rights, migration and poverty.

15

NOW

Siyamiyateliyot (Elizabeth Phillips)

Born: 1939
Birthplace: Seabird Island, British Columbia

When Siyamiyateliyot (Elizabeth Phillips) was just eight years old, she was taken from her family — members of the Stó:lō Nation in British Columbia — and forced to live in a residential school. These schools, sponsored by the Canadian government, separated Indigenous children from their families and communities as a way to strip these children of their Indigenous cultures and assimilate them into white settler society.

At residential school, children were punished for speaking in their Indigenous languages. Language is an important part of any culture; people who speak the same language feel connected to one another. By the time they returned home, many of these children had forgotten the languages vital to their Indigenous identities.

But for the seven years Siyamiyateliyot was at residential school, she held imaginary conversations with her parents in the Halq'eméylem language. This helped her remember the language of her people.

Over time, the number of Halq'eméylem speakers dwindled. By 2018, Siyamiyateliyot was the only person who could speak the language fluently. So professors from the University of British Columbia began working with her to preserve the language. Researchers filmed her speaking and even made an ultrasound recording to see how the muscles in her mouth moved when she made certain sounds.

In June of that year, the University of the Fraser Valley gave Siyamiyateliyot an honorary degree to celebrate her work preserving Stó:lō culture. She gave her acceptance speech in Halq'eméylem.

Shanawdithit

about 1801–1829

Birthplace: Newfoundland

If it weren't for Shanawdithit and her stories and drawings, historians would know almost nothing about her people, the Beothuk. These Indigenous people once lived on Newfoundland. In winter, they hunted animals such as caribou in the island's interior. In spring, they paddled to the coast, where they hunted seal and salmon.

No one knows how many Beothuk people were on Newfoundland when Europeans first met them in 1500. Eventually, European settlers took over more of the island. They brought diseases that the Beothuk people couldn't survive. Trappers and fishers boasted about killing these Indigenous people.

By the time Shanawdithit was born in 1801, there were only about two hundred of her people alive. As she grew up, the population dwindled. In 1823, the British captured Shanawdithit along with her mother and sister, both of whom soon died from tuberculosis (a lung disease). The kidnappers gave Shanawdithit a new name, Nancy April, and moved her to the Exploits Islands, off Newfoundland's coast. She worked there as a servant for five years.

When a search party confirmed that Shanawdithit was the last living Beothuk person, she was moved to the Boeothick (now Beothuk) Institution in St. John's. William Eppes Cormack recorded the stories Shanawdithit told of her culture. She sketched maps of where her people had lived and drew their homes, hunting practices and more.

Shanawdithit died of tuberculosis in 1829. With her death, the Beothuk people and culture were gone. But thanks to her records, they'll never be forgotten.

Wonderful Women!

*The Mary March Provincial Museum is named after Shanawdithit's aunt **Demasduit** (about 1796–1820). She was renamed Mary March by the British. The museum in Grand Falls-Windsor, Newfoundland, houses a collection of Beothuk artifacts.*

17

NOW

Santee Smith
(Tekaronhiáhkhwa)

Born: 1971
Birthplace: Hamilton, Ontario

When she was just two years old, Santee Smith (Tekaronhiáhkhwa) gave her first dance performance. She started ballet at age three. But that year, she broke both her legs — one when a car rolled over it and the other in a bicycle accident. As a young child, Santee also broke her collarbone after falling off her bed. Ballet helped her recover from her injuries and regain her strength.

Santee dreamed of becoming a professional ballerina. At age 11, she was accepted to the National Ballet School in Toronto. She had a hard time leaving her family on the Six Nations of the Grand River reserve near Brantford, Ontario. But it was a step toward achieving her dream.

After training at the school for six years, Santee was conflicted. Ballet was a classical dance style that didn't express her Kanien'kehá:ka (Mohawk) culture. She decided to quit.

Eight years passed, and Santee missed dancing. She wanted to start again, but this time as a choreographer and dancer and in a style inspired by her Indigenous heritage. Finally, she was able to use dance to express herself and her roots.

In 2005, Santee founded the Kaha:wi Dance Theatre. The dancers' performances are bold expressions of Indigenous culture. Today, Santee uses dance to bring attention to issues such as violence against Indigenous women and the trauma of residential schools. Her performance at the 2015 Pan Am Games in Toronto showcased Indigenous cultures. In 2019, Santee was named chancellor (honorary head) of McMaster University.

Karen Kain

Born: 1951
Birthplace: Hamilton, Ontario

THEN

When Karen Kain was eight years old, she wrote, "When I grow up, I am going to be a ballerina." She was inspired after watching Celia Franca, one of the most famous ballerinas in Canada.

At age 11, Karen left home to attend the National Ballet School in Toronto. The change was hard for her, and she was often homesick. When her parents struggled to pay the school fees, Betty Oliphant, the school's founding director, assured them that their money was well spent. She knew Karen was talented. Karen earned a scholarship and was able to stay at the school. Seven years later, she joined the National Ballet of Canada. She was just 18 years old.

Karen wasn't a natural ballerina. She was much taller than the average dancer. As well, her back was too long and her hips weren't flexible enough. But Karen wouldn't accept these limitations. She persisted and soon became a principal dancer and soloist. With her excellent technique, range of movement and skill for interpreting music, Karen was a star in classical and contemporary ballets and won awards around the globe.

In 1997, Karen retired from dancing. She later became the National Ballet of Canada's artistic director — the person who chooses which ballets the company presents and what roles its dancers perform. There are many more men running ballet companies than women, but the situation is changing, thanks to women like Karen. In 2019, Karen became the first Canadian to receive the Queen Elizabeth II Coronation Award. It's presented by Britain's Royal Academy of Dance and is one of the world's top honours for dancers.

DOCTORS

NOW

Samantha Nutt

Born: 1969
Birthplace: Scarborough, Ontario

A visit to Somalia in 1995 changed Samantha Nutt's life. The East African country was in the midst of a war, and Samantha was there as a volunteer doctor to help women and children. She had just graduated from medical school the year before. After seeing the horrors of the war, she knew she would never be the same.

Samantha's path to becoming a doctor wasn't straightforward. In university, she studied drama. Acting taught her a lot about empathy (the ability to understand other people's feelings). When Samantha decided to study medicine, she knew that empathy would help her succeed as a doctor. She earned her medical degree and then took more courses in women's health and healthcare in tropical countries.

Samantha started War Child Canada in 1999, a few years after returning from Somalia. The organization works in countries such as Afghanistan, the Congo and Iraq to help children rebuild their lives after they have been devastated by war or conflict. Workers provide local kids with food, medical care, schooling and counselling. In families that have lost both parents, the older children are given job training so they can support their brothers and sisters. Samantha's work has helped hundreds of thousands of children.

In 2005, *Time* magazine named Samantha one of Canada's five leading activists. Along with her work for War Child Canada, she continues working as a doctor in Toronto. Samantha also teaches medicine at the University of Toronto, reaching the next generation of Canadian doctors.

Emily Stowe

1831–1903
Birthplace: Norwich, Ontario

She was smart enough to become a school principal, but when Emily Stowe decided to become a doctor, Canadian universities refused her — simply because she was a woman.

So Emily went to New York state and graduated as a doctor in 1867. Still, she wasn't allowed to practise legally in Canada. But women wanted her services, so Emily opened an office in Toronto. That made her the first female doctor to practise medicine in Canada.

In the early 1870s, the Toronto School of Medicine reluctantly admitted Emily and Jennie Trout to complete their studies and obtain their Ontario medical licences. The male students left rude notes on the blackboard. Professors tried to embarrass the women with indecent lectures. One day, Emily had enough. She told the professor, "Doctor, if you continue to lecture in this way, I will be repeating every word of what you say to your wife." The professor quickly changed his lecture style.

In 1880, Emily finally was given her Ontario medical licence. To make it easier for other women to become doctors, she opened the Woman's Medical College in Toronto in 1883.

Emily knew changes would only happen for women if politicians had to listen to them. So in 1876, she founded Canada's first suffrage group and, in 1889, founded the Dominion Women's Enfranchisement Association (*suffrage* means the right to vote and *enfranchisement* means granting that right). Although she wouldn't live to see most Canadian women earn the vote in federal elections in 1918, she helped pave the way for that historic day.

MORE AMAZING DOCTORS

1875: Jenny Trout is the first licensed female doctor in Canada.

1883: Augusta Stowe-Gullen, Emily Stowe's daughter, is the first woman to earn her medical degree in Canada.

1885: Sophia B. Jones is the first black woman born in Canada to earn a medical degree.

1903: Irma LeVasseur is the first French-Canadian woman to become a licensed physician.

1909: Bessie T. Pullan is the first Jewish woman to become a doctor in Canada.

1922: Victoria Chung is Canada's first female Chinese doctor.

1998: Cornelia (Nel) Wieman is Canada's first female Indigenous psychiatrist.

NOW

Ayah Bdeir

Born: 1982
Birthplace: Montreal, Quebec

> *The worst thing we can do is say ... "Girls don't like this or that." You never know.*

Sitting in a media lab at one of the world's most prestigious universities, Ayah Bdeir found herself at a crossroads. She had already earned a degree in computer engineering, which made sense — as a kid, she loved taking apart radios and other machines. She had learned programming at age 12. Now, she was in her mid-twenties and studying science at the Massachusetts Institute of Technology (MIT), but she was afraid that she wasn't following her dreams. She also wanted to be an artist.

Ayah wondered if there was a way to use her engineering skills to create art. That's when she came up with the idea for littleBits — small, colourful electric building blocks that snap together with tiny magnets. They can be used to build almost anything, from buzzing toy cars to monsters that light up.

Creating littleBits wasn't easy. Ayah often became frustrated making something that was so new and different, and she gave up on the project many times. After two years of work, she was finally ready to share her idea at the World Maker Faire in New York City. It was a success! In 2011, she launched littleBits as a company.

Ayah wants to give everyone the power to create with electronics. She has even set up a non-profit media lab in Beirut, Lebanon, where she grew up, to encourage people to experiment with art and technology.

Ayah has realized her dream of being an engineer and an artist. She has even had art shows around the world — some including littleBits! Ayah hopes her invention will encourage other artists to innovate.

Elsie MacGill

1905–1980

Birthplace: Vancouver, British Columbia

When Elizabeth "Elsie" Muriel Gregory MacGill was growing up, her family nicknamed her "Miss Fix-It" since she was good at repairing broken lamps and clocks. It was no surprise that she became Canada's first woman to earn a university degree in electrical engineering — the study of electricity and machines.

Elsie was also fascinated by planes and aeronautics (the science of flight), and in 1929, she completed her studies for a master's degree in aeronautical engineering. But before she could graduate, she became infected with polio, a disease that left her physically disabled. When Elsie received her degree later that year, she became the first woman in North America — and likely the world — to be an aeronautical engineer.

Nine years later, Elsie became the world's first woman to design airplanes when she created the Maple Leaf II Trainer. During World War II, she was head of fighter plane production for Canada. Elsie was known as the "Queen of the Hurricanes" because of her work on the Hurricane fighter plane.

After the war, Elsie continued working as an engineer. She also became interested in women's rights, since she had faced discrimination in her own career. In 1967, she travelled across Canada to listen to women's stories of inequality for the Royal Commission on the Status of Women. The Canadian government adopted many of the commission's recommendations, such as paid maternity leave, to improve the lives of Canadian women.

Wonderful Women!

Elsie's mother, **Helen Gregory MacGill** (1864–1947), was one of the first women to graduate from university in Canada. She was also the first female judge in British Columbia.

23

NOW

Melissa Sariffodeen

Born: 1988
Birthplace: London, Ontario

What problems do you want to solve? ... What tools do you want to use? And ultimately, how do you want to change the world?

When Melissa Sariffodeen was just 11 years old, she wanted to build websites from scratch. She taught herself coding so she could write instructions to tell a computer what to do. But Melissa's interest in technology wasn't encouraged at home or in school. She decided to become an accountant, but she didn't enjoy the work.

So in 2011, Melissa cofounded Ladies Learning Code with Breanna Hughes, Heather Payne and Laura Plant. They all wanted to learn more about coding and share those skills with other women. Their goal was to create more equality between men and women in technology.

When the women launched their first workshop, tickets sold out in a day. The second workshop sold out in seven minutes, the third in 30 seconds! Since then, Melissa's organization has taught more than 100 000 Canadians to code.

Now the group is known as Canada Learning Code, with workshops and seminars available to everyone. The organization even runs camps and programs just for kids — Girls Learning Code and Kids Learning Code. Melissa has become known for her strong support of women and young people, and she works hard to increase their confidence and opportunities.

Melissa knows how wonderful it feels to build technology, not just use it. She wants to show women and girls that creating technology isn't intimidating or scary and that it can actually make you feel powerful. She encourages women and girls to set up new businesses and to ask for help when they need it.

Rose Fortune

1774–1864

Birthplace: Philadelphia, Pennsylvania

Born enslaved in the United States, Rose Fortune dreamed of a different life. When the Americans won the American Revolution in 1783, she and her family fled to Annapolis Royal, Nova Scotia. They likely came with the family who owned them and who had been loyal to the British during the war. Rose's family was freed from slavery and became part of the group called the Black Loyalists.

People expected Rose to become a maid or cook. But in 1825, she started her own business. Using a wheelbarrow, she carted luggage between the town's docks and nearby homes and hotels. She was easy to spot, wearing men's heavy work coats and boots.

Gradually, Rose's business grew, and she began to deliver luggage and other cargo all over the town. She also set up a wake-up service to alert travellers so they wouldn't miss their boats.

On the docks, Rose enforced curfews and kept order. She was strong and carried a tall stick for protection. Many people consider her Canada's first unofficial female police officer.

Rose also helped enslaved Americans who were using the Underground Railroad. This was a network of secret routes that enslaved people used to find freedom in Canada. As Rose walked around town, she tapped out messages with her stick to tell people in hiding when it was safe to move. She also drew maps for them on the ground.

In 1841, Rose's delivery service became known as the Lewis Transfer, and horse-drawn carts replaced wheelbarrows. Her descendants continued the business for more than a hundred years.

Wonderful Women!

Rose's descendant **Daurene Lewis** *(1943–2013) was the first black woman to be a mayor in Canada. She was elected in Rose's town, Annapolis Royal, in 1984.*

NOW

Severn Cullis-Suzuki

Born: 1979
Birthplace: Vancouver, British Columbia

> *We're all in this together and should act as one single world toward one single goal.*

Severn Cullis-Suzuki has been an environmentalist her whole life. It's not surprising, since her dad is world-famous environmentalist David Suzuki. She is the author of a number of books about helping the environment. Severn has also co-hosted a nature television series for kids called *Suzuki's Nature Quest* with her dad.

When she was nine years old, Severn founded the Environmental Children's Organization to teach other kids about caring for the planet. Then in 1992, she spoke at the Earth Summit in Rio de Janeiro, Brazil, to give a kid's view of the environmental crisis. Looking out over the audience of business people, diplomats, politicians and reporters from around the world, the 12-year-old cleared her throat nervously. But she was determined to let them know how worried she was about our planet.

Severn told the audience she was afraid to go out in the sun because of the holes in the ozone layer. She said she was fighting for her future and for the future of others on the planet. Severn reminded the officials that kids in kindergarten learn to respect others, to clean up their mess and to share, but that when it comes to the earth, adults have forgotten these lessons. "My father always says, 'You are what you do, not what you say,'" said Severn. "Well, what you do makes me cry at night." The video of her talk, *The Girl Who Silenced the World for Five Minutes*, was shared around the world.

Today, Severn continues to speak out about global environmental problems and also works on local projects that help the planet.

Anahareo (Gertrude Bernard)

1906–1986

Birthplace: Mattawa, Ontario

THEN

Somewhere in my makeup, there is a streak of determined obstinacy.

As a Kanien'kehá:ka (Mohawk) woman, Gertrude Bernard understood that all animals and plants are connected. Her grandmother had shared with her traditional Indigenous teachings about plants and medicine.

In 1925, when Gertrude was 19 years old, she met Grey Owl, a fur trapper from England. He claimed to be descended from the Native American Apache people. He called her Anahareo, which comes from the term *paharomen nahareo*, or "flaming leaf."

Anahareo joined Grey Owl on his trapline but hated killing animals. One day, she saved two beaver kits whose mother had been caught in one of his traps. Grey Owl watched Anahareo raise the little animals. She convinced him to stop trapping and, instead, focus on conservation. Thanks to Anahareo's encouragement, Grey Owl became a bestselling writer and lecturer about the environment.

Strong and independent, Anahareo refused to act the way society expected of women at the time. She wanted to do her own work, not simply support Grey Owl. So she became a prospector, searching for gold and other minerals in northern Ontario and Quebec. Anahareo was likely the first female prospector to travel alone so extensively through the wilderness.

When Grey Owl died in 1938, people discovered he wasn't part Native American as he had claimed. His lie affected how people saw his conservation message and even made them doubt Anahareo's work. She didn't care — she continued to campaign for safer ways to control animal populations and changed people's relationships with nature.

NOW

Susan R. Eaton

Born: 1958
Birthplace: Sydney, Nova Scotia

During a blizzard, Susan Eaton plunged into the water of Halifax Harbour. The 16-year-old was being certified as a scuba diver, and a little cold water couldn't stop her!

Susan loved exploring the ocean — just like her mom, a marine biologist, and her dad, a professional scuba diver. By her late forties, she took up snorkelling because of a heart problem, since staying near the water's surface didn't put as much stress on her heart as deep-sea diving.

Inspired by her love of snorkelling, Susan founded the all-female Sedna Epic Expedition. During the summers of 2014, 2016 and 2018, the women snorkelled through the Arctic Ocean's frigid waters. They were prepared for many challenges: icebergs, polar bears and even the Greenland shark. They also trained for a 3000 km (1864 mi.) snorkel relay through the Northwest Passage — a sea route through the Arctic Ocean. For hundreds of years, thick ice made travelling the passage almost impossible. But climate change is melting the ice so quickly that snorkellers can now swim through the passage using special equipment. The relay expedition aimed to show how global warming is changing our planet.

The expedition is named after Sedna, the Inuit goddess of the sea and mother of all sea mammals. Team Sedna includes Inuit girls, women and Elders who provide insights into Inuit culture and Traditional Knowledge.

Thanks to her explorations of the Arctic and Antarctica, Susan was named one of Canada's 25 greatest female explorers by the Royal Canadian Geographical Society in 2015.

Charlotte Small

1785–1857
Birthplace: Île-à-la-Crosse, Canadian Northwest
(now Saskatchewan)

In the winter of 1805–1806, Charlotte Small, her explorer husband, David Thompson, and his team were snowed in at Reed Lake House, a fur trade post in central Alberta. Food was scarce, and the group faced death by starvation.

Charlotte had many traditional Indigenous skills (her mother was Nehiyaw, or Cree), including finding food in the wilderness. By hunting and trapping enough food for the whole team, Charlotte saved their lives. And she did it all while pregnant and looking after two small children.

Charlotte's husband was one of Canada's most famous explorers and map-makers. During his career, his team — including Charlotte — covered almost 40 000 km (24 855 mi.) across the prairies and Rocky Mountains, as well as navigating the length of the Columbia River in British Columbia. Charlotte walked, rode horseback and canoed across the country, helping to ensure her husband's success.

Many of Canada's explorers depended on Indigenous women like Charlotte to survive. In addition to hunting and trapping, these women translated the languages of the Indigenous people that explorers met. Charlotte also knew which plants were safe to eat and which to use for medicine, and how to make clothes from animal skins.

When David stopped working in 1812, Charlotte may have worried about what was ahead for her. In those times, most European men left their Indigenous wives after retiring. But Charlotte and David moved together to Montreal, where they lived for many years.

THEN

MORE AMAZING EXPLORERS

1889: Mary Schäffer begins exploring the Rocky Mountains and painting the plants that she finds. Mount Schaffer is later named in her honour.

1905: Mina Hubbard leads the winning expedition in a race to map parts of Labrador and Quebec.

1914: Kate Rice explores northern Manitoba and is the first female prospector in northern Canada.

2015: *Canadian Geographic* names **Kathleen Conlan** one of Canada's greatest explorers thanks to her research in the Antarctic and Arctic.

2016: Cave diver **Jill Heinerth** becomes the first Explorer-in-Residence for the Royal Canadian Geographical Society.

NOW

Deepa Mehta

Born: 1950
Birthplace: Amritsar, India

Make the films and tell the stories that move you.

When Deepa Mehta was six years old, she went to a movie theatre for the first time. She cried because she didn't understand why she couldn't smell or touch the people on screen. Her father, who owned the theatre in India, let her touch the film strip. Deepa was amazed — movies seemed like magic to her.

After moving to Canada in 1973, Deepa began making movies about how women see the world. Her movie *Fire* was one of the first Bollywood films to feature a lesbian relationship. When the movie was shown in India, people who were against same-sex relationships fire-bombed theatres. But *Fire* also got people talking about the female characters' lives.

Earth, the next movie in Deepa's Elements trilogy, is about Pakistan separating from India. The final movie in the trilogy, *Water*, is about the abuse of child brides and widows. During filming in India, rioters who believed the film was disrespectful to Hindu culture destroyed the sets. Deepa had to stop production, but eventually she found a place in Sri Lanka to finish the film. In 2007, *Water* was nominated for an Academy Award.

Deepa has also directed, produced and written a comedy. *Bollywood/Hollywood* was released in 2002 and became one of the most successful Canadian movies ever.

Gender inequality happens all around the world, Deepa knows, not just in Eastern countries. She addresses this global problem in her films and also makes sure her female lead actors are paid the same as the male leads. In this way, Deepa is helping to change the film industry.

Judith Crawley

1914–1986
Birthplace: Ottawa, Ontario

In the 1930s, cinema was in its golden age. Movies were now being made with sound and sometimes even in colour. It was an exciting time to be a filmmaker — as Judith Crawley would soon discover.

Judith's husband, Frank Radford "Budge" Crawley, was fascinated by films. So in 1938, while on their honeymoon, they made the documentary *L'Île d'Orléans* about life on this Quebec island. Judith wrote the script and edited the film, and it won Best Amateur Film from the Royal Canadian Geographical Society.

In 1940, Judith directed the film *Four New Apple Dishes,* the first National Film Board of Canada movie ever directed by a woman. She and Budge produced more films from their small apartment. By 1943, they moved their studio into an old church hall in Ottawa and named their production company Crawley Films. They made movies around the world known for their high quality.

In 1948, Judith adapted the Tsimshian legend *The Loon's Necklace.* It was named Film of the Year at the Canadian Film Awards. She was the first woman to win this award. The movie also won the 1950 prize for best North American film at the First International Art Film Festival.

Then Judith focused on producing and writing. She wrote the script for *The Man Who Skied Down Everest,* which won an Academy Award for Best Documentary Feature in 1975. It was the first Canadian movie to win this award.

Over her long career, Judith's many prize-winning films paved the way for female filmmakers and helped the industry take their work more seriously.

Sarah Polley

Born: 1979
Birthplace: Toronto, Ontario

Sarah Polley got her big break when she was just 11 years old. She had already been acting for seven years — it was a natural fit since both her parents worked in the film industry. Now, she was going to star as Sara Stanley in the television series *Road to Avonlea,* based on stories by L. M. Montgomery.

People around the world loved the show, and Sarah was propelled to international fame. In her teens, she starred in a few Hollywood movies. But after encountering harassment and sexism from male filmmakers — and being called "a problem" for speaking out against it — she switched to independent films.

Sarah also became an activist and spoke out about issues that were important to her, such as poverty and social injustice. Then, she realized she could reach people by making her own films. She graduated from the Canadian Film Centre in 2001 and two years later won a Genie Award for her short film *I Shout Love*.

Sarah's movies are often about women searching for their own identities. Her first feature film, *Away from Her*, was based on a short story by Alice Munro. It was nominated for two Academy Awards, including one for Sarah's screenwriting, and won the Genie Award for best directing. For the miniseries *Alias Grace*, based on Margaret Atwood's bestselling novel, Sarah was both producer and screenwriter.

Sarah drew on her experience as an actor to develop her filmmaking style. She also works hard to make sure her movie sets are places where people of all genders can feel comfortable.

MORE AMAZING FILMMAKERS

1921: Nell Shipman is the first Canadian woman to direct a film, *The Girl from God's Country*.

1945: Evelyn Lambart is the first Canadian woman to direct an animated film, *Maps in Action*.

1969: Barbara Wilson's *These Are My People* is the first film directed by an Indigenous woman in Canada.

1977: Claire Prieto's *Some Black Women* is one of the first films made by independent black filmmakers in Canada.

1978: Beverly Shaffer wins an Academy Award for her documentary *I'll Find a Way*.

1987: Patricia Rozema's award-winning *I've Heard the Mermaids Singing* becomes one of the most profitable Canadian films ever made.

1994: Mina Shum makes her popular film *Double Happiness*, a story about a Chinese-Canadian family.

2006: Jennifer Baichwal is the first woman to win the Toronto International Film Festival Award for Best Canadian Feature Film for her movie *Manufactured Landscapes*.

2008: Indigenous filmmaker **Alanis Obomsawin** wins the Governor General's Award for Lifetime Artistic Achievement in film.

2016: Anne Wheeler is the first woman to receive the Directors Guild of Canada Lifetime Achievement Award.

33

NOW

Hayley Todesco

Born: 1996
Birthplace: Calgary, Alberta

When Hayley Todesco was 10 years old, she saw the movie *An Inconvenient Truth.* This film shows how global warming is harming Earth, and it made Hayley want to find ways to slow down climate change and help our planet. But what could she do?

Then Hayley remembered a science demonstration from school. Her class had poured muddy water through a sand filter. They watched as the sand trapped the dirt particles so the water came out clean. Hayley wondered if she could use this idea to invent something to clean up the environment.

Hayley began entering science fairs, each time creating better experiments to help reduce pollution. Growing up in Alberta, she knew about the oil industry and the tailings (toxic oil sands) that are left over after oil is extracted from the ground. Hayley wanted to use sand and bacteria filters to break down the pollutants found in oil sands tailings.

When Hayley was 16 years old, she started building filters using bacteria provided by the University of Calgary, aquarium sand and empty intravenous bags. It took her 120 attempts and two years of work before she knew her invention was a success.

Hayley's bacteria filters can break down the toxic compounds found in oil sands tailings 14 times faster than the current technique of letting them sit in tailings ponds, reducing the time from centuries to decades. With her filters, Hayley beat out students from around the world to win the 2014 Google Science Fair award for her age category.

MORE AMAZING INVENTORS

1870: Jane Campbell is one of the first women listed on a Canadian patent for her invention of "A Machine for Manufacturing Wheels."

1917: Margaret Newton develops wheat varieties that are resistant to the deadly disease wheat rust.

1924: Peg Seller invents synchronized swimming.

1951: Sylvia Fedoruk and her team invent the Cobalt-60 Therapy Unit for treating cancer patients.

1984: At age 12, **Rachel Zimmerman** invents the Blissymbol Printer to help people with physical disabilities communicate.

Susan Olivia Poole

1889–1975
Birthplace: Gaa-waabaabiganikaag
(White Earth Reservation), Minnesota

THEN

Back in 1910, Olivia Poole was desperately trying to get work done around her home in Toronto. But she also had to keep her baby son entertained. It seemed almost impossible, until she remembered what the Anishinaabe (Ojibwe) women did on the reservation where she had grown up.

While a mother was working in the fields, she strapped her baby to a pâhoešestôtse (cradleboard) then hung the baby carrier on a strong tree branch. If the baby cried, her mother would tug on the branch to bounce the baby happily up and down.

Olivia wondered if she could create something similar with items she had around her home. She used a cloth diaper for a seat and hung it from the doorframe using a coiled spring attached to a wooden rod. Her son could push himself off the floor and bounce in his seat. Olivia called her creation the Jolly Jumper. It kept her son happy and developed his leg muscles. Olivia went on to have seven children, and each one loved bouncing in her invention.

It wasn't until the 1950s, after Olivia had moved to Vancouver, that she began making Jolly Jumpers for others — starting with her grandchildren. But she wanted to help even more mothers, so she decided to sell her invention. She received the patent for the Jolly Jumper in 1957.

Olivia's product was a huge success. Within just a few years, one-fifth of all babies in Canada were bouncing in Jolly Jumpers. Today, the Jolly Jumper is one of the world's most famous inventions for babies.

NOW

Sook-Yin Lee

Born: 1966
Birthplace: Vancouver, British Columbia

At 15 years old, Sook-Yin Lee ran away from home. Her parents had just separated, and she could no longer live with her mother, who was physically abusive. Sook-Yin lived on the streets and, eventually, met a group of young artists who introduced her to art and storytelling. This helped her understand her chaotic and unstable childhood and pushed her to become a journalist, storyteller and musician.

After singing in a rock band, Sook-Yin became a television host on MuchMusic in 1995. Her work on the show made her famous all across Canada. As a VJ (video jockey), she interviewed well-known musicians and introduced music videos and live performances. Sook-Yin is bisexual, and she made headlines across the country later that year when she kissed a woman on the air. It was Sook-Yin's way of celebrating the Supreme Court of Canada's decision to protect sexual orientation under the Canadian Charter of Rights and Freedoms.

From 2002 to 2016, Sook-Yin was host of the CBC Radio show *Definitely Not the Opera (DNTO)*. She talked about everything from fear and conflict to food and etiquette. After *DNTO*, Sook-Yin began hosting another CBC radio show, *Sleepover*, which brings together three strangers in each episode to solve a problem from one of their lives.

Through her work as a journalist, actor and filmmaker, Sook-Yin challenges traditional assumptions about gender and sexuality. She is especially interested in stories that explore the challenges that women and immigrants face in society.

Mary Ann Shadd

1823–1893
Birthplace: Wilmington, Delaware

Even as a young child, Mary Ann Shadd knew how important it was to get an education. But in the mid-1800s, it was illegal to educate black people in the state of Delaware, where Mary Ann's family lived. So they moved to Pennsylvania, where she and her brothers and sisters could attend school.

In 1850, the United States passed the Fugitive Slave Act, which threatened all black people with enslavement, even if they had never been enslaved. Mary Ann fled to Windsor, Ontario. There, she set up a school for black children who had escaped to Canada. She encouraged both black and white children to attend her school.

Mary Ann wanted to inspire more black people to move to Canada, where slavery was illegal. So she started the *Provincial Freeman* newspaper in 1853 to publicize the success that black people were having in Canada. Mary Ann knew the paper wouldn't do as well if people were aware it was published by a woman, so she didn't list her name in the paper or take credit for articles she wrote. She was the first black woman in North America to publish a newspaper and one of Canada's first female journalists.

The *Provincial Freeman* told its readers to insist that black people be treated fairly. It supported women's rights and publicized the work of local women's organizations. Mary Ann was criticized by both black people and white people for her opinions, but she kept publishing. She encouraged black people to become educated and worked hard to change how white people saw black people who had been enslaved.

You have a right to your freedom and to every other privilege connected with it.

NOW

Denise Dwyer

Born: 1963
Birthplace: Manchester, England

In the summer of 1973, 10-year-old Denise Dwyer was heading outside to play. But before she made it to the door, her father called her back to watch what was unfolding on television. It was one of the hearings for the Watergate scandal — a major political event in the United States that would lead to President Nixon's resignation. Denise's father was unimpressed by one of the lawyers. He told his daughter that she could do a better job as a lawyer one day.

Denise's family had moved to Canada from England four years earlier. They often talked about justice, equality and race and even had a copy of the Canadian Charter of Rights and Freedoms in their living room. It was no wonder that Denise became a lawyer in 1991.

After working as a lawyer for many years, Denise wanted to find a way to make the law profession more inclusive and diverse. So in 2006, she started the Black Female Lawyers Network (also called Sistahs-in-Law). The group gives black women in law a place to talk about their experiences of discrimination due to their race or gender.

Denise loved mentoring women and became more interested in education. She had always believed that education could help people achieve their goals, no matter their skin colour. So in 2016, she joined Ontario's Ministry of Education. She wants teachers and students to know more about traditions and histories from many diverse cultures — especially those of black and Indigenous people. Her work helps to make schools more inclusive and equal for everyone.

MORE AMAZING LAWYERS

1897: Clara Brett Martin is the first female lawyer in the British Empire.

1946: Gretta Wong Grant is the first Chinese-Canadian woman to practise law.

1976: Roberta Jamieson is the first Indigenous woman to earn a law degree in Canada.

1982: Bertha Wilson is the first woman appointed to the Supreme Court of Canada.

2000: Beverley McLachlin is the first female Chief Justice of Canada.

2004: Rosalie Silberman Abella is the first Jewish woman appointed to the Supreme Court of Canada.

Violet King Henry

1929–1982

Birthplace: Calgary, Alberta

THEN

Today about half of all law school graduates in Canada are women. But when Violet King Henry graduated from the University of Alberta's law school in 1953, she was the only woman in her class. She was also the first black woman to become a lawyer in Canada.

Back in high school, Violet had written in her yearbook that she dreamed of becoming a lawyer. But it took determination to make her dream come true. Her university workload was heavy, and Violet had to teach piano to pay for her schooling. Still, she made time to be a student leader both on campus and in a national group of university students. Violet was also a member of a university feminist group that discussed history and current events.

A few years after Violet began practising law, she moved to Ottawa to work for the government's citizenship and immigration department. Violet travelled around the country to meet community leaders and talk about the racism they witnessed. With her help, the department worked to stop discrimination and help Canadians respect everyone's rights.

Violet moved to the United States in 1963 and began working for the Young Men's Christian Association (YMCA). There she focused on helping black people find work, and in 1976, she became the first woman named to a top position at the YMCA.

Violet once said she felt that any woman who wasn't white had to work especially hard to get a job. But she hoped this would change and that, one day, women would be judged on their ability, rather than their race and gender.

NOW

Whatever you want to excel in, make sure it is something that ... leaves you with a feeling of wonder at the marvellousness of the universe.

Karen Yeats

Born: 1980
Birthplace: Halifax, Nova Scotia

When Karen Yeats was growing up, she couldn't decide between a career in math or music. She loved the beauty of writing music — but she also loved entering math contests. The more competitions Karen entered, the more experience she got and the better she became at math. Soon, she was competing across Canada and even internationally.

Because of her success in these high-level tournaments, Karen chose to study mathematics at the University of Waterloo in 1998. She had already learned how to apply math using calculations and equations. But now, she was studying theoretical mathematics. Mathematicians say that theoretical math makes real-life math make sense.

When Karen graduated in 2003, she won a Governor General's Silver Medal as the top math student in Canada. Few women have won this award for mathematics. That same year, she received an honourable mention for the prestigious Morgan Prize — a top mathematics award in North America. Only one other Canadian woman had ever achieved this honour.

Five years later, Karen earned a Ph.D. in math from Boston College in Massachusetts. She then went on to become a Canada Research Chair at the University of Waterloo. Only about one-third of these positions are held by women, but Karen's success is helping to change that. In 2016, she became one of the few Canadian women awarded a Humboldt Research Fellowship to study math in Berlin, Germany.

Karen has long felt that math is more than just useful. She believes that it's beautiful and elegant, just like music.

Cecilia Krieger

1894–1974

Birthplace: Jasło, Galicia (now part of Poland)

Cecilia Krieger was born in Poland to a Jewish family. In 1919, she began studying math and physics at the University of Vienna in nearby Austria. But Jewish people were being persecuted in Europe, so a year later, Cecilia, her sisters and her mother fled to Canada.

Cecilia began studying at the University of Toronto even though she knew very little English. She took private lessons to learn the language while studying mathematics.

Despite this challenge, Cecilia earned a bachelor of arts degree in 1924 and a master of arts degree a year later. And Cecilia continued studying. In 1930, she received her Ph.D. She was the first Canadian woman to earn a Ph.D. in mathematics from a Canadian university.

In 1931, Cecilia became a lecturer at the University of Toronto. It took 10 years for her to be named an assistant professor because women at the university were often overlooked for promotions. Cecilia wanted to help other women in math. So she held get-togethers where female math students could meet. She also helped them apply for scholarships.

Especially known for her work in topology (the study of the properties of geometric shapes), Cecilia also studied trigonometry (the area of math that focuses on the relationships between the sides and angles of triangles).

In 1995, the Canadian Mathematical Society created the Krieger-Nelson Prize to honour Cecilia. The award is given to women who are involved in groundbreaking mathematical research.

Wonderful Women!

The Krieger-Nelson Prize is named after Cecilia and another top Canadian mathematician, **Evelyn Nelson** *(1943–1987). Evelyn was well known for her contributions to algebra (the study of math symbols and how they are used).*

41

NOW

Jennie Carignan

Born: 1968
Birthplace: Asbestos, Quebec

When Jennie Carignan was young, she dreamed of being a dancer. She began studying ballet and jazz when she was eight years old. But Jennie also knew how to cut wood and fire a shotgun alongside her brothers and father. Her parents never told her there were activities she couldn't do just because she was a girl.

The sense of purpose and challenge Jennie saw in the military appealed to her, and in 1986, she joined the Canadian Armed Forces. She was just 17 years old. Women had first been admitted to the Royal Military College of Canada (the Armed Forces' college) only seven years earlier.

Training was tough. Instruction was in English, and Jennie only spoke French. But she was a fast learner and was soon promoted. Jennie was one of the first women to train as a combat engineer, which meant she would be on the front lines of battle. This job, and many others, didn't become available to women in the Canadian Armed Forces until 1989.

Jennie's career with the Armed Forces has taken her to some of the world's most dangerous war zones. In 2002, she served in Bosnia-Herzegovina, where she cleared explosive devices from farmers' fields. Jennie also fought in the war in Afghanistan from 2009 to 2010. In June 2016, Jennie became a brigadier general. She was the first woman promoted to this rank from a combat role.

Today, Jennie still makes time for dancing, but now she loves the elegance and grace of Flamenco (a type of Spanish dancing). She continues to bring the discipline and energy of dance to her work.

Michelle Douglas

Born: 1963
Birthplace: Ottawa, Ontario

When Michelle Douglas joined the Canadian military in 1986, she wasn't planning to make history. She just wanted to serve her community and country.

Michelle worked hard and soon was promoted to the Special Investigations Unit. One of the unit's jobs was to identify gay and lesbian soldiers and have them dismissed from the military. In those days, the military did not allow people who were openly LGBTQ+ to serve.

As one of the first female officers appointed to this unit, Michelle was determined to do a good job. But that meant hiding the fact that she was a lesbian. When word leaked out about her sexual orientation, Michelle was questioned for two days. Eventually, she disclosed she was a lesbian. She was discharged in 1989 from the Armed Forces — it said she was "not advantageously employable due to homosexuality," even though she had an excellent work report and was often at the top of her class.

Michelle felt she was being treated unfairly, so she launched a lawsuit against Canada's Department of National Defence in 1990. In 1992, just before Michelle's case went to trial, the Canadian military changed its policy of banning gay and lesbian people from the military. Michelle had changed the Armed Forces forever. For Canada, it was an important step toward becoming a more open and inclusive country.

Now Michelle is a human rights activist and works with LGBTQ+ refugees. She also helped create the Foundation for Equal Families, a group that aims to achieve equal rights for same-sex couples.

Any time you can end discrimination as a matter of policy, it is a huge victory.

NOW

I don't feel brave because I sing about dating a girl ... For me, bravery is being a doctor or a teacher or a politician.

Tegan and Sara

Born: 1980
Birthplace: Calgary, Alberta

Identical twin sisters Tegan and Sara Quin began playing guitar and writing songs when they were 15 years old. A few years later, they used their school's recording studio to make their first demo album. The sisters' band was originally called Sara and Tegan. But people kept thinking the duo was a solo performer named Sara Antegan. When they swapped their names to Tegan and Sara, there was no more confusion. Their songs started to climb the charts.

Their music has since won many awards and has been featured on television shows and in movies — you've probably sung along to their song "Everything Is Awesome!!!" from *The Lego Movie*. Tegan and Sara have headlined at such music festivals as Coachella, Lollapalooza and SXSW (South by Southwest). They also performed at the closing ceremony for WorldPride Toronto in 2014.

Both Tegan and Sara are lesbian, so advocating for LGBTQ+ equality is especially important to them. They promote marriage equality for everyone. In 2016, they founded the Tegan and Sara Foundation to help support issues important to LGBTQ+ girls and women. The sisters also donate money and fundraise for other gay rights causes and organizations.

In 2018, the twins met with Prime Minister Justin Trudeau and members of parliament to encourage them to improve rights for LGBTQ+ girls and women in Canada. Tegan and Sara want the government to address issues that affect LGBTQ+ communities, such as discrimination, mental health and underemployment.

Portia White

1911–1968

Birthplace: Truro, Nova Scotia

The first black Canadian opera singer to earn international fame, Portia White is considered one of the world's best classical singers of the 1900s. She had a deep contralto, or alto, voice — the lowest vocal range for women.

Portia began singing in her church choir at age six. Two years later, she was singing opera. She was so determined to become a professional singer that she walked 16 km (10 mi.) each week for music lessons.

In the early 1930s, Portia taught school in Africville, a small black community in Halifax. She won a scholarship to continue studying music in 1939, and in just two years, she was singing across Canada. She sang European classics, spirituals and gospel music, but had trouble booking gigs simply because she was black.

Portia persevered, and gradually her audiences grew. In 1944, she sang in New York City. Despite the positive reviews and packed audiences, she wasn't welcome in some restaurants and hotels because of her skin colour. Portia chose to ignore the racism with quiet dignity.

Problems with her voice forced Portia to retire at the age of 41. She became a singing teacher in Toronto, working with many top Canadian performers. Portia still gave a few more concerts, including one for Queen Elizabeth II in 1964.

Portia's legacy lives on today. The Nova Scotia government created the Portia White Prize to honour professional Nova Scotian artists. Portia is also the first black Canadian woman to be declared "a person of national historic significance" by the government of Canada.

First you dream, then you lace up your boots.

NOW

Penny Oleksiak

Born: 2000
Birthplace: Toronto, Ontario

Most athletes begin practising their sport when they are very young. But Penny Oleksiak didn't learn to swim until she was nine years old. When she applied to train with swimming clubs, she was turned down again and again because she couldn't even swim the length of a pool.

Eventually, Penny was able to start training because swim coaches saw that she loved to race. Her style was poor at first, but she asked lots of questions about how to become a better swimmer. She applied the information her coaches taught her, kept improving and was determined to win every race she entered. As well, Penny was growing — she's now 186 cm (6 ft. 1 in.) tall — and her long legs and arms helped rocket her through the water.

At one practice when Penny was 13 years old, her swim club was sharing the pool with a top national swim team. The team's coach noticed Penny's tenacity and offered to work with her. Penny trained hard, and a few years later, she qualified for the 2016 Summer Olympic Games.

Penny had never competed at the Olympics before. She was just 16 years old. But she won a gold medal in the 100 m freestyle and silver in the 100 m butterfly. And with her teammates, she won bronze medals in both freestyle relay events.

Those results made Penny Canada's youngest Olympic gold medallist and the first Canadian to win four medals at a single Summer Games. Only cyclist and speed skater Clara Hughes and speed skater Cindy Klassen have won more Olympic medals than Penny. But Penny has many more Olympic Games ahead of her!

Fanny "Bobbie" Rosenfeld

1904–1969

Birthplace: Ekaterinoslav, Russia

(now Dnipro, Ukraine)

In the early 1900s, doctors and coaches thought women were too fragile to be athletes. Although the modern Olympic Games began in 1896, it wasn't until 1928 that women were allowed to compete in track and field. Fanny "Bobbie" Rosenfeld was there, and she showed just how strong women can be.

Nicknamed Bobbie because of her short, bobbed hairstyle, this amazing athlete excelled at basketball, hockey, softball, tennis and many other sports, all without ever having a coach. She was also an incredible runner.

At the 1928 Olympics, Bobbie headed the small but talented Canadian women's team, called the Matchless Six. She won gold in the 400 m relay and silver in the 100 m race. She scored more points than any athlete — male or female — and led the Matchless Six to first place.

When one of her teammates, Jean Thompson, hurt her leg just before a race, Bobbie entered the same event to run alongside Jean and encourage her. Although the distance was much longer than Bobbie usually ran, she knew Jean needed help. The pair finished fourth and fifth. People said that Bobbie could have won a medal, but she refused to pass Jean.

Five years later, severe arthritis ended Bobbie's athletic career. For the next 20 years, she was a sportswriter, known for her clever, funny style. She celebrated pioneering female athletes and broke down barriers for women in sports. Bobbie was named Canada's Female Athlete of the First Half-Century (1900 to 1950) by Canada's Sports Hall of Fame. Each year, Canada's top female athlete wins the Bobbie Rosenfeld Award.

47

THEN+NOW

Clara Hughes

Born: 1972
Birthplace: Winnipeg, Manitoba

It takes a determined athlete to compete in both the Summer and Winter Olympic Games. Clara Hughes had that determination. She competed as a cyclist in the Summer Games and a speed skater in the Winter Games.

When Clara was a young teen, she never thought of herself as an athlete. Then she saw Canadian speed skater Gaétan Boucher compete. Clara took up the sport at age 16. A year later, she began cycling.

Clara's courage, willpower and desire to succeed have taken her to the top. In 1996, she became the first Canadian woman to win an Olympic medal in road cycling (she won two bronze medals that year). In speed skating, Clara won Olympic bronze in 2002, silver and gold in 2006, and bronze in 2010. She is tied with Cindy Klassen as the Canadian athlete with the most Olympic medals. She's also the only athlete to win multiple medals in both games.

In 2012, Clara retired from Olympic competition and now focuses on helping others. Although she is known for her wide smile, Clara has suffered from depression. As a spokesperson for Bell Canada's Let's Talk program, she works to end the stigma around mental illness. In 2014, she completed Clara's Big Ride, a 110-day bicycle tour across Canada to raise awareness about mental health.

Clara is also involved in Right To Play, a worldwide organization that uses play to educate and empower children facing adversity. As well, she is an Honorary Witness for the Truth and Reconciliation Commission, helping to improve relations between Indigenous and non-Indigenous Canadians.

MORE AMAZING OLYMPIANS

1924: Figure skater **Cecil Smith** is the first woman to represent Canada at the Olympics.

1928: Ethel Calderwood, of the Matchless Six, becomes the first Canadian woman to win Olympic gold (she wins for high jump).

1948: Barbara Ann Scott earns Canada's first Olympic gold in figure skating.

1968: Skier **Nancy Greene** wins two medals at the Winter Games, a first for a Canadian woman.

1968: Elaine "Mighty Mouse" Tanner-Watt is Canada's first female medalist in Olympic swimming.

1976: Susan Nattrass competes against men in trap shooting. She is the first female competitor in an Olympic shooting event.

1984: Lori Fung wins gold in a new event: rhythmic gymnastics.

1988: Synchronized swimmer **Carolyn Waldo-Baltzer** is the first Canadian woman to win two gold medals at the same Olympic Games.

1998: Women's curling debuts at the Olympics, and **Sandra Schmirler** leads the Canadians to gold.

1998: Women first compete in Olympic ice hockey. The Canadian team, led by **Stacy Wilson**, wins silver.

2008: Carol Huynh earns Canada's first gold medal in women's Olympic wrestling.

2010: Tessa Virtue and skating partner **Scott Moir** are the first North Americans to win Olympic gold for ice dance.

2015: Tricia Smith, an Olympic rower, is the first female president of the Canadian Olympic Committee.

NOW

Christi Belcourt

Born: 1966
Birthplace: Scarborough, Ontario

One of the world's most famous Métis artists, Christi Belcourt is inspired by the land. Like many Indigenous artists, she fills her work with symbols and themes that show a respect for, and connection to, the earth.

Christi is best known for her acrylic paintings. They are influenced by traditional floral beadwork, an important skill and livelihood for many Indigenous women. Through her art, Christi explores subjects such as the environment and Indigenous rights. Her vibrant paintings often focus on complex issues, such as identity, culture, racism and discrimination, and the divisions they create between people.

Indigenous women's rights are also important to Christi. She wanted to find a way to honour missing and murdered Indigenous women and their families. So in 2012, she started the art project *Walking with Our Sisters*. The floor installation is made up of more than 1800 pairs of moccasin vamps (the tops of shoes) — one pair for each woman. The vamps were beaded by people across Canada and around the world. The incomplete moccasins represent how the lives of these women are unfinished.

Christi has been involved in many other art projects. She designed the medals for the 2015 Pan Am Games in Toronto. She has even worked with Valentino, a high-fashion Italian design house, with her art inspiring the fabric for a clothing line.

You can see Christi's art in galleries across Canada, including the National Gallery of Canada (NGC) in Ottawa. She has won many awards, including a Governor General's Innovation Award.

MORE AMAZING ARTISTS

1880: Painter **Charlotte Schreiber** is the first woman elected to the Royal Canadian Academy of Arts.

1896: Mary Augusta Hiester Reid is the first female painter to have her own exhibit in Canada.

1942: During the Second World War, **Molly Lamb Bobak** becomes Canada's first female war artist.

1971: Joyce Wieland is the first living Canadian woman to have a solo exhibit at the NGC.

1979: Lynn Johnston's famous comic strip, *For Better or For Worse*, first appears in newspapers.

2009: Daphne Odjig is the first Indigenous woman to exhibit solo at the NGC.

Emily Carr

1871–1945

Birthplace: Victoria, British Columbia

Emily Carr often shocked her family and hometown of Victoria. In the late 1800s, painting was considered a nice hobby for proper young ladies, but not a serious career. But Emily longed to paint — not gentle landscapes, but the lush wilderness of British Columbia's coast. In 1898, she began painting Indigenous people in Ucluelet and even Alaska.

At age 18, Emily studied art in San Francisco, and then in England and France. While in Paris, she developed her distinctive style of painting.

When Emily returned to Victoria in 1912, she decided to paint the mostly abandoned Gitxsan, Haida and Tsimshian villages on the coast. She wanted to sketch them before they disappeared. They would inspire her for the rest of her life.

Emily's paintings were considered too unusual to sell, so to earn a living — and feed her many pets — she became a landlady. That left little time for painting. But in 1927, members of the Group of Seven, Canada's most famous group of painters, saw her art and encouraged her. Emily became famous for painting trees, shores and skies that shimmered with energy.

After a heart attack in 1937, Emily was told to cut back on painting. So she turned to writing. Her first book, *Klee Wyck*, won the Governor General's Literary Award. *Klee wyck* means "laughing one" and is the name the Nuu'chah'nulth (Nootka) First Nation gave Emily.

Emily battled many obstacles that women of her time faced and she changed how people saw British Columbia's rugged coast. She's still considered one of the top artists in Canadian history.

THEN

Do not try to do extraordinary things, but do ordinary things with intensity.

NOW

Aurélie Rivard

Born: 1996
Birthplace: Saint-Jean-sur-Richelieu, Quebec

Aurélie Rivard loved swimming from a young age. As a kid, she wanted to be a lifeguard, but she was too young. So she kept swimming at a nearby public pool just for fun. After a coach noticed her determination and potential, Aurélie began training. She entered her first swimming competition when she was 11 years old.

Aurélie was born with an impairment to her left hand. Her friends at school and her twin sister, Charlotte, always treated her the same as everyone else. But in high school, when Aurélie switched to a new school to focus on swimming, the kids weren't so kind. Aurélie began believing the cruel things people said about how her impairment made her different. Her passion for swimming helped Aurélie regain her self-confidence.

When Aurélie was just 16 years old, she competed in her first Paralympic Games. She took home the silver medal in the 400 m freestyle S10 ("S10" describes the competitors' level of physical impairment). At the 2015 Parapan Am Games, Aurélie earned six gold medals and one silver — that's more medals than any other female athlete in the history of the Games.

Then at the 2016 Paralympic Games, Aurélie won three gold medals and a silver medal — more than any Canadian Paralympian ever. She even set two world records (in the 50 m and 400 m swims) and a Paralympic record (in the 100 m swim).

No wonder Aurélie has been named Swimming Canada's female Para-swimmer of the year for three years in a row!

Chantal Petitclerc

Born: 1969

Birthplace: Saint-Marc-des-Carrières, Quebec

THEN

When a barn door fell on Chantal Petitclerc at age 13, she became paralyzed from the waist down. Until then, she hadn't been athletic, but Chantal decided to stay in shape at the rehabilitation centre's pool. Swimming boosted her confidence and made her realize how much she liked a challenge. A wheelchair racing coach noticed Chantal's determination and suggested she try the sport.

A wheelchair racer has to have more than strong arms to succeed — she also needs a strong spirit. At first, competitions scared Chantal, but she persisted and overcame her fear. In 1992, she began winning medals at the Paralympic Games. She has since won many Paralympic medals, including five at both the 2004 and 2008 Games.

Chantal had unusually quick reflexes and was known for her explosive starts. She had great technique and was extremely disciplined. She had to be: her coach lived in Ottawa while Chantal lived in Montreal, so most of her training was done alone. They kept in contact by email and phone. Thanks to Chantal's versatility — she competed in distances ranging from sprints to marathons — she was one of Canada's top medal-winners.

Chantal retired from racing in 2008 and eight years later was named to the Senate of Canada. Her main priorities are health, the importance of sports and the rights of people with disabilities. Chantal remembers how she searched for a female role model when she was an athlete, but never found one. So she always makes time to speak to young women with disabilities who ask for advice.

You have to be ready to take risks. Don't be afraid to fail sometimes. Failure, after all, is what gives value to success.

NOW

Rupi Kaur

Born: 1992
Birthplace: Hoshiarpur, India

Poetry is like holding up a mirror and seeing myself.

Rupi Kaur's family moved from India to Brampton, Ontario, when she was four years old. The move to Canada was a huge culture shock for her. She couldn't speak English, so her mother encouraged her to draw and paint to communicate with the kids at school. Eventually, Rupi's English improved, and she was soon writing poems to give to her friends.

By her early 20s, Rupi was sharing her poems on social media. She posted them on Tumblr and Instagram with black-and-white drawings, and became known as an Instapoet (a poet who publishes mostly on Instagram). Rupi published her first book, *milk and honey*, in 2014. It has sold more than 2.5 million copies and has been translated into more than 30 languages. Few poets sell that many books. Her second book, *the sun and her flowers*, was also an instant bestseller.

All of Rupi's poems are written in lowercase, and the only punctuation she uses is the period. She formats her work this way to show respect for her Sikh roots — Gurmukhi, a Sikh script, uses the same style.

Rupi's writing is minimal and straightforward. In her work, she often focuses on themes such as love, femininity, abuse and healing. One of Rupi's most famous poems challenges the social taboos around menstruation. Her writing also emphasizes that the ordinary experiences of women, especially minority women, shouldn't be ignored.

In 2018, Rupi toured North America, reading her poems to packed concert halls. She captivated audiences with both her words and the way she performed her work.

Pauline Johnson (Tekahionwake)

1861–1913

Birthplace: Six Nations Indian Reserve
(now Six Nations of the Grand River), Ontario

A little more than one hundred years ago, Emily Pauline Johnson was Canada's most popular poet and entertainer. Billing herself as the Mohawk Princess because her father was a Kanien'kehá:ka (Mohawk) chief, she toured Canada, Britain and the United States, reading her poetry and talking about Canada and the rights of Indigenous people.

Ever since she was a child, Pauline had been writing poetry. She was the first Indigenous poet published in Canada, but she had limited success until she began giving readings. With their strong, swinging rhythms, Pauline's poems sounded especially good read aloud.

Pauline knew how to attract a crowd and keep its attention. She performed her poems with a dramatic flair. People swarmed to see her, even though they were sometimes shocked when she demanded better treatment for Indigenous people. At the time, people did not expect women to speak their minds.

To emphasize her Kanien'kehá:ka heritage, Pauline wore buckskin with her father's hunting knives hanging from her waist. She called herself Tekahionwake, which means "double wampum" in Kanien'kehá. (Wampum are shell beads used as decoration or for currency, or to signify treaties when woven into a belt.)

Pauline was one of the few women of her time to make a living from writing and performing. She retired to Vancouver in 1909, and her funeral four years later was the largest the city had ever seen. Pauline is the only person to be buried in Stanley Park, which was her favourite place in Vancouver.

THEN

My aim, my joy, my pride is to sing the glories of my own people.

NOW

MORE AMAZING POLITICIANS

1921: Agnes Macphail is the first woman elected to parliament.

1930: Cairine Wilson is Canada's first female senator.

1972: Rosemary Brown is the first black woman to win a provincial election in Canada.

1983: Jeanne Sauvé is the first female Governor General.

1988: Ethel Blondin-Andrew is the first Indigenous woman elected to parliament.

1993: Kim Campbell is Canada's first female prime minister.

Julie Lemieux

Born: 1972
Birthplace: Drummondville, Quebec

When voters in Très-Saint-Rédempteur, Quebec, elected Julie Lemieux as their mayor on November 5, 2017, they made history. Not only was she the first female mayor for this small village near Montreal, but she was also the first openly transgender mayor in Canada.

Julie was born with a boy's body, but she knew around age six that she felt more feminine than masculine. She began transitioning when she was 29 years old.

Eight years later, Julie moved to Très-Saint-Rédempteur. There, she became interested in politics when she joined others trying to save the local church from demolition. Thanks to the group's work, the church was turned into a community centre. The experience showed Julie the importance of being involved in the community. In 2013, she ran to be a municipal councillor and won.

When Julie decided to run for mayor four years later, she didn't make her identity as a trans woman part of her campaign. She wanted people to recognize her skills, not focus on her gender. Instead, Julie campaigned on the importance of change. She also stressed improving communications between the residents and the people they elect. Some of her opponents' supporters tried to marginalize her during the campaign because of her gender identity, but they didn't succeed. Voters knew Julie was transgender, and she never felt they discriminated against her.

On election day, Julie won by a wide margin — 48 percent of the vote! She appreciates the people of Très-Saint-Rédempteur for their acceptance and openness.

The Famous Five

1927–1929
Place of formation: Edmonton, Alberta

No woman in the entire British Empire had ever been a magistrate (a type of judge) until Emily Murphy became one in 1916. But on her first day, a lawyer told her she had no right to be there, just because she was a woman.

A year later, Canadian women were pressuring the prime minister to make Emily a senator. But again, some people opposed the idea and argued that when the British North America Act (BNA Act) talked of "persons" being appointed to the Senate, it meant men, not women.

Emily decided things had to change. She discovered she needed five people to challenge the BNA Act. So in 1927, she formed a group with Louise McKinney, Nellie McClung, Henrietta Muir Edwards and Irene Parlby. They would become known as the Famous Five. They sent a petition to Canada's Supreme Court, the country's top law court, asking if the word *persons* in the BNA Act included women. The Court said no — the term *persons* did not include women.

The Famous Five didn't give up. They took the "Persons Case," as it was called, to the Privy Council of England, Canada's highest court at the time. On October 18, 1929, the Council said that the word *persons* in the BNA Act should include both men *and* women. Finally, most Canadian women were eligible to be appointed to the Senate. The next year, Cairine Wilson became the first female senator in Canada.

In honour of the Famous Five, the Governor General's Awards in Commemoration of the Persons Case are awarded every year. They celebrate Canadians who improve gender equality.

Emily Murphy
(1868–1933)

Louise McKinney
(1868–1931)

Nellie McClung
(1873–1951)

Henrietta Muir Edwards
(1849–1931)

Irene Parlby
(1868–1965)

NOW

Nivatha Balendra

Born: 1995
Birthplace: Montreal, Quebec

There are so many amazing women in science in the past ... who are inspiring me, inspiring other girls to continue.

When Nivatha Balendra heard that there are about 14 000 oil spills in the world every year, she felt she had to do something. But it was the oil spill resulting from a deadly train wreck in Lac-Mégantic, Quebec, on July 6, 2013, that really spurred Nivatha to take action. She saw how this devastating accident affected not only the environment, but also the people and city.

At university, Nivatha had already studied micro-organisms (really small organisms, such as bacteria) and how they can clean up pollution. She knew some bacteria produce compounds called biosurfactants. These substances break down and disperse hydrocarbons, which are the basis of all oils. Nivatha wondered if bacteria could be used for cleaning up oil spills.

Nivatha wanted to talk about her idea with other scientists. But because she was so young, people ignored her emails, and her requests for information were denied. Instead of giving up, these rejections made her more determined.

So Nivatha went looking for bacteria to work with and was shocked to discover a new strain of *Pseudomonas fluorescens* in her own backyard. This bacteria could degrade oil and provide an environmentally safe solution to oil contamination. In 2018, Nivatha founded the company Dispersa Inc. to create products for cleaning up oil spill sites.

Nivatha is also the founder of the International Young Scientists Mentorship Program. She believes no one's too young to make a difference and that girls should be proud to be passionate about science.

Harriet Brooks Pitcher

THEN

1876–1933

Birthplace: Exeter, Ontario

Harriet Brooks Pitcher lived at a time when it was difficult for women to get an education. There were few women going to university, but Harriet was smart and won scholarships. In 1894, she began studying at McGill University in Montreal.

After graduating in 1898, Harriet began researching radioactivity with Ernest Rutherford, known as the father of nuclear physics. She was Canada's first female nuclear physicist.

Harriet studied radioactive elements. (An element is a substance made of only one kind of atom.) She proved one element could change into another — scientists had been sure this was impossible. As well, she helped identify the radioactive element radon. And in 1903, Harriet discovered that when a radioactive atom emits a particle, the atom springs back, or recoils. This became known as recoil theory, which is still important today.

In 1904, Harriet began teaching at Barnard College in New York. But after Harriet got engaged, the dean demanded that Harriet resign. The college did not allow married women to work there. Harriet felt a duty to show that women have a right to both a career and marriage. Both she and the female head of the department pleaded to the dean, but they couldn't change her mind. Harriet broke off her engagement but still decided to resign.

Harriet travelled to Europe in 1906 to work with British physicist J. J. Thomson, who discovered the electron. When she married Frank Pitcher in 1907, Harriet gave up physics. But she accomplished more in a few years than many scientists do in a lifetime.

Wonderful Women!

*When Harriet was in Europe, she worked with **Marie Curie** (1867–1934) in Paris, France. Marie is the world's most famous female physicist.*

NOW

Dionne Brand

Born: 1953
Birthplace: Guayaguayare, Trinidad and Tobago

As a young girl growing up in Trinidad, Dionne Brand already knew she wanted to be a writer. She submitted her writing to local newspapers using the pen name Xavier Simone. She chose the name because she was inspired by black jazz singer Nina Simone, whose songs she listened to late at night on the radio.

In 1970, when Dionne was 17 years old, she came to Canada to study at the University of Toronto. At that time, there were few groups in the city for young black writers to share their work, so Dionne created some. Several years later, in 1986, she founded *Our Lives*, Canada's first newspaper especially for black women.

No Language Is Neutral, Dionne's breakout poetry book, was published in 1990. Told from a black feminist perspective, it explores issues of immigration and identity. Seven years later, Dionne won the Governor General's Literary Award for her poetry book *Land to Light On*. She is also known for her fiction and nonfiction books. One of her best-known novels is *What We All Long For*. From 2009 to 2012, she was Toronto's poet laureate (a poet chosen to write for special occasions).

Dionne's writing is beautiful, lyrical and innovative. It's full of vivid imagery to help readers understand the experiences and emotions of her characters. She uses her writing to explore the place of black women in Canada. Dionne hopes that her writing can help break down barriers around gender and race. As a social activist and lesbian, she also speaks out about discrimination against the LGBTQ+ community.

L. M. Montgomery

1874–1942

Birthplace: Clifton (now New London),
Prince Edward Island

When Lucy Maud Montgomery received Charlottetown's *Daily Patriot* newspaper on November 26, 1890, she was thrilled. There was one of her poems — in print for the first time! She was just 16 years old.

Maud (she hated being called Lucy) kept writing poems and short stories while working as a teacher and for a newspaper. By 1905, she decided to make writing her only job. But she had still never written a book.

Then one day, she was looking through an old notebook filled with story ideas. She found this note: "Elderly couple apply to orphan asylum for a boy. By mistake a girl is sent them." Immediately, Maud imagined what this girl was like. Her name even popped into Maud's head: Anne-with-an-e. Maud liked her character so much that she decided to write a book about her.

It took Maud months to write Anne's story, fitting it in between her other writing and chores. She finished the manuscript in October 1905 and sent it to a publisher — only to receive a swift rejection. After the fifth rejection, she sadly put her book away. Months later, while cleaning out a cupboard, she came across the manuscript and decided to submit it once more. Finally, it was accepted!

That book, *Anne of Green Gables*, was published in 1908. Maud would write seven more books about Anne, as well as other novels, short stories and poems. Her stories have been made into movies, television shows, plays and musicals. More than a hundred years later, Maud's first book is still a bestseller and a beloved classic for fans all over the world.

Down, deep down, under all the discouragement and rebuff, I knew I would "arrive" some day.

Margaret Atwood

Born: 1939

Birthplace: Ottawa, Ontario

Ever since Margaret Atwood was a teenager, she's been writing. When she started publishing back in the 1960s, few writers were telling stories from a Canadian point of view. Margaret wanted to change that.

Her first book, a work of poetry, was published in 1961. Five years later, Margaret's second poetry book, *The Circle Game,* won the Governor General's Literary Award. Margaret then began writing novels. *The Handmaid's Tale*, one of her most famous books, is a dark, futuristic story about women's lives. It won the Governor General's Literary Award in 1985 and has been turned into a television series, a play, a film, an opera and a ballet.

Margaret is one of Canada's most beloved writers. Her books have won prizes around the world. She's known for her strong characters, precise language and startling images. An important theme for her is survival. That may be because Margaret spent her childhood summers in the wilderness of northern Ontario and Quebec. Her work also shines a light on how the world sees women.

Today, Margaret is also known for her activism. Women's issues and the environment are just two of the topics she comments on in newspapers and on social media. As well, she fights censorship and defends writers' rights around the world.

Margaret is an inventor, too. She created the robotic LongPen, which lets authors sign their books from anywhere in the world. And she's the first author to contribute to the Future Library project — her book *Scribbler Moon* will be published in the year 2114!

MORE AMAZING WRITERS

1824: Julia Catherine Hart is the first person born in what is now Canada to publish a novel.

1852: Susanna Moodie's classic *Roughing It in the Bush* is a first-hand account of settler life.

1852: Catharine Parr Traill's *Canadian Crusoes* is the first Canadian adventure novel for kids.

1884: Marie-Louise-Félicité Angers, writing under the name Laure Conan, is French Canada's first female novelist.

1894: Margaret Marshall Saunders's *Beautiful Joe* is the first Canadian book to sell more than one million copies.

1899: Winnifred Eaton is the first Asian novelist published in North America.

1937: Laura Salverson is the first woman to win the Governor General's Literary Award.

1947: French-Canadian writer **Gabrielle Roy** wins the Governor General's Literary Award for her first book, *Bonheur d'occasion* (*The Tin Flute*).

1973: Métis author **Maria Campbell** publishes *Halfbreed*, an important work of Indigenous literature.

1984: Mitiarjuk Nappaaluk is the first woman to publish a novel in Inuktitut.

1995: Carol Shields is the first Canadian to win the prestigious Pulitzer Prize for Fiction.

2013: Alice Munro wins Canada's first Nobel Prize in Literature.

FOLLOW *in Her* FOOTSTEPS

How will you be inspired by the women you read about in this book? Like them, you have the power to make your community, your country — even the world — a better place for everyone to live.

What are you passionate about?

Hayley Todesco (page 34) is passionate about the environment. Her invention can help break down the harmful pollutants found in oil sands.

What achievement would make you a trailblazer?

Violet King Henry (page 39) was a trailblazer when she became the first black female lawyer in Canada.

Where can you look for inspiration?

Inspired by the pâhoešestôtse (cradleboard) from her Anishinaabe culture, Susan Olivia Poole (page 35) invented the Jolly Jumper.

Who are your role models?

Roberta Bondar (page 13) was the first Canadian woman in space and a role model for astronaut Jennifer Sidey-Gibbons (page 12).

What makes you feel brave?

Lilly Singh (page 8) imagined she had an invisible *S* on her chest like a superhero. It gave her the courage to believe she could do anything.

Is there something happening in the world that you think is unfair?

Michelle Douglas (page 43) was treated unfairly when she was discriminated against for her sexual orientation. She helped to make the Canadian military more inclusive for LGBTQ+ people.

How can you overcome obstacles in your life?

Aurélie Rivard (page 52) overcame the unkind things kids said about her physical impairment. Her love of swimming helped Aurélie regain her self-confidence and become a top Paralympic athlete.

How can you find persistence when someone tells you, "You can't"?

Lucy Maud Montgomery's (page 61) *Anne of Green Gables* was rejected five times by publishers. Because of Maud's persistence, her book was eventually published and became a beloved classic around the world.

More INSPIRING Canadian WOMEN

Eva Aariak (1955–) became the first female premier of Nunavut in 2008. Earlier, as the first languages commissioner for Nunavut, she had to choose an Inuktitut word for *Internet*. She picked *ikiaqqivik*, which means "travelling through layers." The name is based on the Inuit idea of shamans moving through time and space looking for answers.

Maude Abbott (1869–1940) was a top student but was denied entry into medical school because she was a woman. She persisted and graduated as a doctor in 1894. Maude became famous for her heart research. In 1906, she founded the International Association of Medical Museums, now called the International Academy of Pathology.

"One of my daydreams, which I feel to be selfish, is that of going to school."
— *Maude Abbott*

Louise Arbour (1947–) is a lawyer and judge who helps people around the world whose human rights have been abused. In 2004, she became the first Canadian appointed as high commissioner for human rights at the United Nations (UN). Louise was then appointed as UN special representative for international migration in 2017 to help refugees and migrants.

Elizabeth Arden (1878–1966) made makeup available to women through her cosmetics empire, at a time when makeup was mostly used for the theatre. Born Florence Nightingale Graham, after the famous nurse, she changed her name upon moving to New York. Elizabeth introduced eye makeup to North American women and pioneered the idea of the makeover in her salon. Her drive, business smarts and ability to spot trends made her a worldwide success and multi-millionaire.

"It is remarkable what a woman can accomplish with just a little ambition."
— *Elizabeth Arden*

Kenojuak Ashevak (1927–2013) introduced Inuit art to the world and is one of Canada's most beloved printmakers. She grew up sewing beautiful designs on sealskin. Then in the late 1950s, she was given her first piece of paper to draw on. Her bold early drawings often showed birds and mammals changing into other animals. Kenojuak's *The Enchanted Owl* is one of the most famous works of Inuit art.

"There is no word for art. We say it is to transfer something from the real to the unreal." — *Kenojuak Ashevak*

Pitseolak Ashoona (about 1904–1983)

is one of the world's best-known Inuit artists. Her lively prints, showing the traditional ways of her people, often feature monsters and spirits, and have been sold around the globe. Pitseolak inspired her granddaughters, artists Shuvinai Ashoona (1961–) and Annie Pootoogook (1969–2016), who are famous for their depictions of modern Inuit life.

"If no one tells me to stop, I shall make [prints] as long as I am well. If I can, I'll make them even after I'm dead."

— *Pitseolak Ashoona*

Jean Augustine (1937–) became

Canada's first black woman elected as a member of parliament (MP) in 1993. She was also the first black female cabinet minister (advisor to the prime minister). Thanks to Jean, February is known as Black History Month in Canada. She focused on multiculturalism and women's rights until she retired as an MP in 2006.

"Black history is not just for black people — black history is Canadian history." — *Jean Augustine*

Mary Rose-Anna Bolduc (1894–1941),

better known as La Bolduc, is often considered Quebec's first singer-songwriter. A record she released in 1929 sold 12 000 copies — no one had ever sold that many records in the province. People loved her upbeat, funny songs, which combined traditional folk music from both Ireland and Quebec.

Phyllis Bomberry (1943–2019)

played award-winning softball for 25 years. In 1968, this catcher became the first woman to win the Tom Longboat Award. The prize is named in honour of the famous long-distance runner and is given to top Indigenous athletes. Phyllis was inducted into the Softball Canada Hall of Fame in 2009.

Molly Brant (Konwatsi'tsiaiénni)

(about 1736–1796) is one of the most significant people in North American Indigenous history. A Kanien'kehá:ka (Mohawk) woman, she was head of the Six Nations matrons, a powerful group of women who chose the chiefs of the Iroquois Confederacy (a First Nations government). During the American Revolution, Molly urged Six Nations people to remain loyal to Britain.

Deanna "Dee" Brasseur (1953–)

joined the Canadian Armed Forces in 1972, when most women in the military were secretaries or nurses. In 1981, she became one of the first three female pilots in the Canadian Forces and, later, one of two women in the world (along with Canadian Jane Foster) to operate a fighter jet. Deanna speaks out against sexual abuse in the Forces, following her own experience.

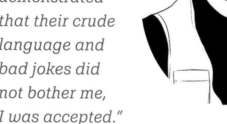

"Once I had established my credibility ... and demonstrated that their crude language and bad jokes did not bother me, I was accepted."

— *Deanna Brasseur*

Measha Brueggergosman

(1977–) began her singing career in her local church choir. Today, this award-winning opera singer and concert artist is known for her incredible range, dramatic performances and powerful voice. She has sung around the world, including at the opening ceremony of the 2010 Winter Olympics in Vancouver.

"I have to make my contribution a hopeful one. I can't see the world any other way."

— *Measha Brueggergosman*

Thérèse Casgrain (1896–1981) led the

fight that earned Quebec women the right to vote in 1940. In 1951, she was chosen to head the Co-operative Commonwealth Federation (later the New Democratic Party) in Quebec, becoming the first woman ever to lead a political party in Canada. Thérèse was appointed to the Senate in 1970.

Adrienne Clarkson (1939–) became the

second female Governor General of Canada in 1999. An Asian-Canadian woman, she was the first visible minority appointed to the position. Previously, Adrienne had worked as a magazine and television journalist. She cofounded the Institute for Canadian Citizenship in 2005 to help new citizens become a part of Canadian society.

Charmaine Crooks (1962–) was the

first Canadian woman to compete in five Olympic Games for track and field. In 1994, she became Canada's first woman to run the 800 m race in less than two minutes. Charmaine works with Peace and Sport, an international organization that uses sport to build inclusive communities and help bring peace to the world.

Céline Dion (1968–) is famous for her romantic ballads, powerful voice, discipline and determination. Not only is she Canada's bestselling singer, but with more than 200 million albums sold worldwide, Céline is one of the bestselling musicians in the world. She has won 20 Juno Awards and 5 Grammys, and her recording of "My Heart Will Go On" from the movie *Titanic* won an Academy Award.

"I'm from Quebec, and every time I go to a country, I say that. It's my roots, my origins, and it's the most important thing to me." — Céline Dion

Mary Two-Axe Earley (1911–1996) was a Kanien'kehá:ka (Mohawk) activist who fought for the rights of Indigenous women. Her work led to changes to the Indian Act (a set of laws governing Indigenous people) to correct its discrimination against Indigenous women. A strong speaker, Mary gave talks around the world, calling for justice, human rights and women's equality.

Ursula Franklin (1921–2016) was a physicist who developed a field of science called archaeometry, which uses scientific techniques to date ancient artifacts. During World War II, she was imprisoned in a Nazi work camp. She later campaigned against war and spoke out against nuclear weapons.

"Peace is not the absence of war — peace is the absence of fear."
— Ursula Franklin

Biruté Galdikas (1946–) is the world's expert on orangutans. Before she began studying these endangered apes, little was known about them, since they live mostly in the treetops of isolated forests in Borneo and Sumatra, in Indonesia. Biruté campaigns for conservation of orangutans and the preservation of their rainforest habitat.

Helen Hogg (1905–1993) greatly increased scientists' knowledge about the age and position of stars. This astronomer was a top expert on globular star clusters (groups of stars that are the oldest objects in our galaxy, the Milky Way). Helen mentored other women and inspired them to become scientists. Through her writing and radio and television broadcasts, she helped people learn about the stars.

Barbara Howard (1920–2017) became one of the fastest women in the British Empire when, at age 17, she broke the record for the 100-yard dash.

She then raced at the British Empire Games in 1938 in Australia, helping Canada's relay teams win silver and bronze medals. This sprinter was likely the first black woman to represent Canada at an international sports competition.

Idle No More (founded 2012) is an Indigenous rights movement established by four women: Jessica Gordon (Pasqua First Nation), Sylvia McAdam (Nehiyaw, or Cree), Sheelah McLean (non-Indigenous) and Nina Wilson (Kahkewistahaw First Nation). They started this grassroots movement to fight government abuses of Indigenous rights, with round dances, blockades of rail lines and more.

Jane Jacobs (1916–2006) organized people to protect their neighbourhoods from development. This urban activist worked hard to cancel downtown expressways.

In her popular books, Jane explained how to make cities work for the people who live there. Jane's Walks are held in more than 200 cities around the world to show people the importance of her ideas.

Angela James (1964–) had a tough hockey style and a powerful shot. She played from 1980 to 2000 and was called the first superstar of modern women's hockey. Angela helped Canada's national women's hockey team win world championships in 1990, 1992, 1994 and 1997. When she was inducted into the Hockey Hall of Fame in 2010, Angela was the first openly gay player, one of the first women and only the second black athlete to be included.

Michaëlle Jean (1957–) was a journalist who became the first black person on French-Canadian television news. Then in 2005, she was named Canada's first black Governor General and she focused her efforts on the Canadian Forces, Indigenous people and the arts. Ten years later, Michaëlle became the first female secretary-general of the International Organisation of La Francophonie, a group of countries where French is spoken.

"Empower women and you will see a decrease in poverty, illiteracy, disease and violence."
— *Michaëlle Jean*

Elsie Knott (1922–1995) served as chief of Ontario's Curve Lake First Nation. When elected in 1954, she was Canada's first woman chosen to be chief of a First Nation. Elsie worked hard to preserve the Anishinaabemowin (Ojibwe) language, revive powwow celebrations and improve access to education for First Nations kids.

k.d. lang (1961–) is a pop and country singer-songwriter, known for her powerful voice and wide vocal range. She has won nine Juno Awards and four Grammy Awards, sung with many music legends and helped raise the profile of Canadian female singers. As a gay woman, k.d. is an activist for LGBTQ+ equality.

"Every single person in this nation has the right to be themselves."
— *k.d. lang*

Margaret Laurence (1926–1987) wrote award-winning books and short stories for adults and children. She began writing in her teens, and her powerful work would become known for its realistic dialogue and sensitivity to people who are cut off from society. Margaret was also an advocate for the environment, literacy and peace.

Maud Lewis (1903–1970) was one of Canada's most famous folk artists. Her colourful paintings depict scenes of everyday life in rural Nova Scotia. Maud was born with several physical disabilities and later developed rheumatoid arthritis, which made it difficult for her to move her hands. Still, Maud painted almost every surface of her home!

"As long as I've got a brush in front of me, I'm all right."
— *Maud Lewis*

Kay Livingstone (1918–1975) was a social activist, radio broadcaster and actor who fought for the rights of black women. She came up with the term *visible minority* to refer to non-white people (not including Indigenous people). Kay was the first president of the Canadian Negro Women's Association and, in 1973, helped set up the first National Congress of Black Women.

Jeanne Mance (1606–1673) sailed from

France to New France (now Quebec) in 1641, making her one of Canada's first female settlers. She helped found the city of Montreal and was the colony's official treasurer. As New France's first nurse, Jeanne was also the founder and director of the Hôtel-Dieu de Montréal — the first hospital in Canada.

Frances McGill (1882–1959) became

Saskatchewan's provincial pathologist in 1922, which made her the province's expert on diseases. Nicknamed the "Sherlock Holmes of Saskatchewan," this forensic pathologist deduced the cause of death in many murder cases. In 1946, Frances became the first woman named Honorary Surgeon to the Royal Canadian Mounted Police, the highest honour the RCMP has given to a woman.

Sarah McLachlan (1968–) is known

for her emotional lyrics, beautiful melodies and high vocal range. This singer-songwriter has won many international music awards and sold more than 50 million albums. From 1997 to 1999, Sarah organized Lilith Fair, an all-female music festival. One of the most successful concert tours ever, it raised $10 million for charities.

"We're constantly being told what other people think we are, and that's why it is so important to know yourself."
— *Sarah McLachlan*

Joni Mitchell (1943–) is considered one of

the world's greatest singer-songwriters. A folk, pop and jazz singer, she's known for her unique guitar style, moving lyrics and breezy voice. Joni has won many international music awards and influenced singers such as Sarah McLachlan (bottom left). Environmental awareness is important to Joni — just listen to her song "Big Yellow Taxi."

"When the world becomes a massive mess with nobody at the helm, it's time for artists to make their mark."
— *Joni Mitchell*

Sandra Lovelace Nicholas (1948–)

is a Wolastoqiyik (Maliseet) activist. In 1985, she helped rewrite the Indian Act so women would no longer lose their Indigenous Status after marrying a non-Status person. (Indigenous men never lost their Status after marriage.) Twenty years later, Sandra became Canada's first Indigenous woman appointed to the Senate.

"We, the Native women, feel no one should have the right to discriminate."
— *Sandra Lovelace Nicholas*

Ellen Page

Ellen Page (1987–) began acting professionally at age 10. Her breakthrough role in the 2007 film *Juno* earned her an Academy Award nomination and made her an international star. She has since appeared in many blockbusters, including two X-Men movies, in which she plays the superhero Kitty Pryde. Since coming out in 2014, Ellen has been an outspoken advocate for LGBTQ+ rights.

"We deserve to experience love fully, equally, without shame and without compromise." — Ellen Page

Georgina Pope

Georgina Pope (1862–1938) was a nurse in the South African (Boer) War. For her service, she was awarded Canada's first Royal Red Cross medal in 1903. At the time, women were only permitted in the military as nurses, and Georgina helped ensure they were given an officer rank in the Canadian Army Medical Corps (CAMC). In 1908, Georgina became the first head of the CAMC's nursing service.

Vivienne Poy

Vivienne Poy (1941–) became the first Asian-Canadian senator in 1998. She sat in the Senate for 14 years, focusing on gender issues, multiculturalism, immigration and human rights. Because of Vivienne, Canadians celebrate Asian Heritage Month every May. She is also a well-known fashion designer and author, as well as sister-in-law to Adrienne Clarkson (page 68).

Buffy Sainte-Marie

Buffy Sainte-Marie (1941–) is one of Canada's most beloved singer-songwriters. She recorded her first album in 1964 and has since won many awards for her music. Of Nehiyaw (Cree) descent, Buffy is also a social activist who focuses on Indigenous issues and advocates for peace. In 1997, she founded the Cradleboard Teaching Project to help people better understand Indigenous issues.

"It's time for a far greater awareness of what women have done and what we're capable of doing." — Buffy Sainte-Marie

Idola Saint-Jean

Idola Saint-Jean (1880–1945) was a journalist, educator and women's rights activist. Thanks to her work, and that of Thérèse Casgrain (page 68), Quebec women were granted the provincial vote in 1940 (that's 22 years after women had earned the federal vote). The Prix Idola St-Jean is awarded to women who improve life for Quebec's women.

Laura Secord (1775–1868) became a hero in the War of 1812, a war between the United States and Britain for control of Canada. Laura overheard American officers' plans for a surprise attack and walked 32 km (20 mi.) through the wilderness to warn the British. She saved the Niagara area in Ontario from being taken over by the Americans.

Bev Sellars (1955–) was chief of the Xatśūll First Nation at Soda Creek, British Columbia, for more than 10 years. She is also known for her memoir, *They Called Me Number One,* which describes her terrible experience of being ripped from her family and culture and placed in a residential school. Through her writing, she helped people understand the atrocities of the residential school system.

Donna Strickland (1959–) is the third woman to win the Nobel Prize in physics. She's the second Canadian woman to win a Nobel Prize (after Alice Munro, who won in literature). Donna's a pioneer in the field of pulsed lasers, ones that produce intense short bursts of laser light. Techniques Donna helped develop are used in eye surgery.

Tanya Tagaq (1975–) combines traditional Inuit throat singing with classical, electronic, punk and rock music. Inuit throat singing is usually performed as a duet by two women, but Tanya developed her own one-woman version. This experimental musician has won many awards, including Juno Awards and the Polaris Prize, and is known for her intense live performances. As a musician, painter and writer, she is one of many new cutting-edge Indigenous artists in Canada.

"We're not a culture from the past. We've amalgamated and we're part of everything. We can't be pushed away anymore."
— *Tanya Tagaq*

Thanadelthur (about 1697–1717) brought peace between her people, the Denesuline (Chipewyan), and the Nehiyaw (Cree) people in the territory that's now known as Manitoba. Because she was courageous, smart and strong, and knew many languages, this translator and mediator was also a helpful guide to fur traders working for the Hudson's Bay Company (HBC) in the early 1700s. Thanadelthur's name means "marten shake" in Denesuline (a marten is a furry mammal), but HBC records call her the "Ambassadress of Peace."

Shania Twain (1965–) is not only the
bestselling female country singer ever, she's also one of the bestselling musicians of all time. Thanks to songs like "Man! I Feel Like a Woman" and "That Don't Impress Me Much," she has sold more than 85 million records. Shania had to retire from singing for eight years due to illness but returned to performing in 2012.

"It's important to give it all you have while you have the chance."
— Shania Twain

Irene Uchida (1917–2013) was one of the
first Canadians to work in cytogenetics. This field of science studies chromosomes, the tiny structures inside cells made from DNA. Irene analyzed chromosomes to predict disorders, such as Down syndrome, that are caused by abnormal genes. She became world-famous for her research, particularly on the side effects of X-rays on the human body.

Sheila Watt-Cloutier (1953–) has
received recognition around the world for her work fighting climate change and supporting human rights. A strong negotiator, this Inuit environmental activist also works hard to preserve her people's culture. As international chair of the Inuit Circumpolar Council, she was one of the only Indigenous women involved in the organization.

Hayley Wickenheiser (1978–) played
with Canada's national women's hockey team for 23 years and scored more points than any other player. She participated in five Winter Olympic Games and one Summer Olympic Games (playing softball) and also played in a men's semi-professional hockey league in Finland. Many consider Hayley the greatest female hockey player in history. She was inducted into the Hockey Hall of Fame in 2019.

"People would say, 'Girls don't play hockey. Girls don't skate.' I would say, 'Watch this.'"
— Hayley Wickenheiser

Alice Wilson (1881–1964) was Canada's
first female geologist (a scientist who studies Earth's history, especially as recorded in rocks). She became world-famous for her knowledge of the fossils and rocks in the Ottawa area. Alice became a university lecturer and mentor to geology students. She also wrote a children's book to help interest kids in geology.

Important Dates in Canadian Women's History

Long before settler societies: Women hold powerful political roles in many Indigenous communities, such as the Haudenosaunee (Iroquois) and Kanien'kehá:ka (Mohawk) First Nations.

1791–1834 Women who own property can vote in Lower Canada (part of today's Quebec and Labrador).

1862 The first female university students in Canada attend Mount Allison University.

1867 Canada is formed under the British North America Act. Under the new act, women are not allowed to vote.

1869 Indigenous women with Indian Status lose their Status when marrying non-Indigenous men due to the Gradual Enfranchisement Act.

1876 The Indian Act diminishes the traditional roles of women in many Indigenous communities.

1876 The Toronto Women's Literary Club is founded by Emily Stowe (page 21) and daughter Augusta Stowe-Gullen (page 21). The name deliberately hides the organization's purpose: to earn women the vote. It is renamed the Toronto Women's Suffrage Association in 1883.

1883 Woman's Medical College opens in Toronto for women who want to study and teach medicine.

1893 The National Council of Women of Canada is founded by Lady Ishbel Aberdeen. The organization works for women's social rights and, by 1910, for women's right to vote.

1897 The Women's Institute is founded by Adelaide Hoodless and Erland Lee to educate women living in rural communities.

1900 Most women who own property can vote in municipal elections.

1914–1918 More than 3100 women serve as nurses during World War I. Military nurses get the vote in 1917. On the home front, more than 30 000 women work in factories and offices and on farms, while men are fighting overseas.

1916 Most women can vote in provincial/territorial elections in Manitoba, Saskatchewan and Alberta, followed by:
1917 British Columbia and Ontario
1918 Nova Scotia
1919 New Brunswick and Yukon Territory
1922 Prince Edward Island
1925 Newfoundland, including present-day Labrador
1940 Quebec
1951 Northwest Territories, including present-day Nunavut

1918 Most Canadian women get the vote in federal elections. Asian women get the vote in 1948, Inuit women in 1953 and all Indigenous women in 1960.

1929 The Famous Five (page 57) win the "Persons Case," which states that Canadian women can become senators.

1939–1945 More than 50 000 women serve in the armed forces during World War II.

1956 The Female Employees Equal Pay Act ensures equal pay for women who perform work similar to men.

1964 Bill 16 is passed, allowing women in Quebec to sign a lease or open a bank account without their husband's signature.

1967 The Royal Commission on the Status of Women is formed to address such issues as equal pay, maternity leave, daycare, birth control, abortion and women's representation in government. It also addresses issues specific to Indigenous women.

1969 Birth control and same-sex relationships are legalized.

1971 The Canadian government adds a minister on the status of women to promote women's equality.

1971 The Native Women's Association of Canada is established to attain equality for Indigenous women, predominantly First Nations and Métis women.

1971 The Canadian government grants women paid maternity leave.

1973 The Canadian Advisory Council on the Status of Women is created (disbanded in 1995).

1974 The Royal Canadian Mounted Police accepts its first female recruits.

1974 The National Film Board of Canada creates Studio D, the world's first government-funded film production group for female filmmakers. The studio goes on to win three Academy Awards.

1975 International Women's Day is first celebrated on March 8.

1977 The Canadian Human Rights Act makes discrimination against women illegal. An amendment in 1983 makes sexual harassment illegal, as well as discrimination based on pregnancy or marriage. In 1996, discrimination based on sexual orientation is outlawed.

1978 The Canada Labour Code is changed so that women can no longer be fired for being pregnant.

1982 The Canadian Charter of Rights and Freedoms protects women's rights and outlaws discrimination based on sex, physical or mental ability, ethnicity, religion or age.

1984 The organization Pauktuutit is founded to promote Inuit women's rights.

1985 The Indian Act is amended to restore Status to Indigenous women who lost their Status by marrying non-Indigenous men.

1989 On December 6, an armed man kills 14 women at the École Polytechnique in Montreal after calling them feminists. In 1991, the White Ribbon Campaign is launched to end male violence against women. December 6 is declared the National Day of Remembrance and Action on Violence Against Women.

1992 Women's History Month is celebrated for the first time in October.

2005 Same-sex marriage is legalized.

2008 The Feminist History Society is formed to create a written record of the women's movement in Canada over the last 50 years.

2012 The International Day of the Girl Child, October 11, is declared by the United Nations and recognized for the first time in Canada and around the world.

2015 The Canadian government launches the National Inquiry into Missing and Murdered Indigenous Women and Girls.

2015 The Canadian government, under Prime Minister Justin Trudeau, has an equal number of women and men as cabinet ministers for the first time in history.

2017 Women's March Canada, a walk for women's equality, takes place on January 21 in 38 communities across the country.

2017 The #MeToo movement gives women in Canada and around the world a voice to speak out against sexual harassment.

RESOURCES

Further Reading

Butts, Edward. *She Dared: True Stories of Heroines, Scoundrels, and Renegades*. Toronto: Tundra Books, 2005.

Dalrymple, Lisa. *Fierce: Women Who Shaped Canada*. Toronto: Scholastic Canada, 2019.

Fournel, Kelly. *Great Women from Our First Nations*. Toronto: Second Story Press, 2007.

Kyi, Tanya Lloyd. *Canadian Girls Who Rocked the World*. Vancouver: Whitecap Books, 2011.

Author's Selected Sources

Books

Forster, Merna. *100 Canadian Heroines: Famous and Forgotten Faces*. Toronto: Dundurn Press, 2004.

Forster, Merna. *100 More Canadian Heroines: Famous and Forgotten Faces*. Toronto: Dundurn Press, 2011.

Johnston, David, and Tom Jenkins. *Ingenious: How Canadian Innovators Made the World Smarter, Smaller, Kinder, Safer, Healthier, Wealthier, and Happier*. Toronto: McClelland & Stewart, 2017.

Lennox, Doug. *Now You Know Canada's Heroes*. Toronto: Dundurn Press, 2009.

Martin, Sandra. *Working the Dead Beat: 50 Lives that Changed Canada*. Toronto: House of Anansi Press, 2012.

Sherwood, George. *Legends in Their Time: Young Heroes and Victims of Canada*. Toronto: Dundurn Press, 2006.

Simoni, Suzanne. *Fantastic Female Filmmakers*. Toronto: Second Story Press, 2008.

Wolfe, Margie. *150 Fascinating Facts About Canadian Women*. Toronto: Second Story Press, 2017.

Websites

A Mighty Girl
www.amightygirl.com

The Canadian Encyclopedia
www.thecanadianencyclopedia.ca

"Canada's Great Women," Canada's History
www.canadashistory.ca/explore/women/canada-s-great-women

Dictionary of Canadian Biography
www.biographi.ca

"Heritage Minutes," Historica Canada
www.historicacanada.ca/heritageminutes

Heroines.ca
www.heroines.ca

Library and Archives Canada
www.bac-lac.gc.ca

Films

Trecartin, F. Whitman, dir. *Rhythm Stick to Freedom*. Edmonton: Great North Productions, 1998.

Ness, Mitchell, dir. *The Canadians*, "Pauline: The Pauline Johnson Story." Toronto: Smoke Lake Productions, 1999.

INDEX

Aariak, Eva, 66
Abbott, Maude, 66
Abella, Rosalie Silberman, 38
Anahareo (Gertrude Bernard), 27
Angers, Marie-Louise-Félicité (Laure Conan), 62
Arbour, Louise, 66
Arden, Elizabeth (Florence Nightingale Graham), 66
Ashevak, Kenojuak, 66
Ashoona, Pitseolak, 67
Ashoona, Shuvinai, 67
Atwood, Margaret, 32, 62–63
Augustine, Jean, 67

Baichwal, Jennifer, 32
Balendra, Nivatha, 58
Bdeir, Ayah, 22
Belcourt, Christi, 50
Best, Carrie, 7
Blondin-Andrew, Ethel, 56
Bobak, Molly Lamb, 50
Bolduc, Mary Rose-Anna (La Bolduc), 67
Bomberry, Phyllis, 67
Bondar, Roberta, 12, 13, 64
Brand, Dionne, 60
Brant, Molly (Konwatsi'tsiaiénni), 67
Brasseur, Deanna, 68
Brooks Pitcher, Harriet, 59
Brown, Rosemary, 56
Brueggergosman, Measha, 68

Calderwood, Ethel, 49
Campbell, Jane, 34
Campbell, Kim, 56
Campbell, Maria, 62
Carignan, Jennie, 42
Carr, Emily, 51
Casgrain, Thérèse, 68, 73
Chung, Victoria, 21
Clarkson, Adrienne, 68, 73
Conlan, Kathleen, 29
Crawley, Judith, 31
Crooks, Charmaine, 68
Cullis-Suzuki, Severn, 26

Demasduit (Mary March), 17
Desmond, Viola, 7
Dion, Céline, 69
Douglas, Michelle, 43, 64
Dwyer, Denise, 38

Earley, Mary Two-Axe, 69
Eaton, Susan R., 28
Eaton, Winnifred, 62
Edwards, Henrietta Muir, 57

Famous Five, the, 57, 76
Fedoruk, Sylvia, 34
Fortune, Rose, 25
Foster, Jane, 68
Franklin, Ursula, 69
Fung, Lori, 49

Galdikas, Biruté, 69
Grant, Gretta Wong, 38
Greene, Nancy, 49

Hart, Julia Catherine, 62
Heinerth, Jill, 29
Herman, Erma, 13
Hill, Esther Marjorie, 11
Hill, Jennie Stork, 11
Hogg, Helen, 69
Howard, Barbara, 70
Hubbard, Mina, 29
Hughes, Clara, 46, 48–49
Huynh, Carol, 49

Idle No More, 70

Jacobs, Jane, 70
James, Angela, 70
Jamieson, Roberta, 38
Jean, Michaëlle, 70
Johnson, Pauline (Tekahionwake), 55
Johnston, Lynn, 50
Jones, Sophia B., 21

Kain, Karen, 19
Katta, Anjali, 6
Kaur, Rupi, 54
King Henry, Violet, 39, 64
Knott, Elsie, 71
Krieger, Cecilia, 41

Lambart, Evelyn, 32
lang, k.d., 71
Laurence, Margaret, 71
LeVasseur, Irma, 21
Lee, Sook-Yin, 36
Lemieux, Julie, 56
Lewis, Daurene, 25
Lewis, Maud, 71
Livingstone, Kay, 71
Lovelace Nicholas, Sandra, 72

MacGill, Elsie, 23
MacGill, Helen Gregory, 23
Macphail, Agnes, 56
Mance, Jeanne, 72
Martin, Clara Brett, 38
McClung, Nellie, 5, 57
McGill, Frances, 72
McKinney, Louise, 57
McLachlan, Sarah, 72
McLachlin, Beverley, 38
Mehta, Deepa, 30
Mitchell, Joni, 72
Montgomery, L. M., 32, 61, 64
Moodie, Susanna, 62
Munro, Alice, 32, 62, 74
Murphy, Emily, 57

Nappaaluk, Mitiarjuk, 62
Nattrass, Susan, 49
Nelson, Evelyn, 41
Newton, Margaret, 34
Nutt, Samantha, 20

Obomsawin, Alanis, 32
Odjig, Daphne, 50
Oleksiak, Penny, 46
Oliphant, Betty, 19

Page, Ellen, 73
Parlby, Irene, 57
Payette, Julie, 14–15
Petitclerc, Chantal, 53
Pickford, Mary (Gladys Louise Smith), 9
Polley, Sarah, 32–33
Poole, Susan Olivia, 35, 64
Pootoogook, Annie, 67
Pope, Georgina, 73
Poy, Vivienne, 73
Prieto, Claire, 32
Pullan, Bessie T., 21

Reid, Mary Augusta Hiester, 50
Rice, Kate, 29
Rivard, Aurélie, 52, 64
Rosenfeld, Fanny "Bobbie," 47
Roy, Gabrielle, 62
Rozema, Patricia, 32

Sainte-Marie, Buffy, 73
Saint-Jean, Idola, 73
Salverson, Laura, 62
Sariffodeen, Melissa, 24
Saunders, Margaret Marshall, 62
Sauvé, Jeanne, 56

Schäffer, Mary, 29
Schmirler, Sandra, 49
Schreiber, Charlotte, 50
Scott, Barbara Ann, 49
Secord, Laura, 74
Sellars, Bev, 74
Seller, Peg, 34
Shadd, Mary Ann, 37
Shaffer, Beverly, 32
Shanawdithit (Nancy April), 17
Shields, Carol, 62
Shim, Brigitte, 10
Shipman, Nell, 32
Shum, Mina, 32
Sidey-Gibbons, Jennifer, 12, 64
Singh, Lilly, 8, 64
Siyamiyateliyot (Elizabeth Phillips), 16
Small, Charlotte, 29
Smith, Cecil, 49
Smith, Santee (Tekaronhiáhkhwa), 18
Smith, Tricia, 49
Stowe, Emily, 21, 76
Stowe-Gullen, Augusta, 21, 76
Strickland, Donna, 74

Tagaq, Tanya, 74
Tanner-Watt, Elaine, 49
Tegan and Sara, 44
Thanadelthur, 74
Todesco, Hayley, 34, 64
Traill, Catharine Parr, 62
Trout, Jenny, 21
Twain, Shania, 75

Uchida, Irene, 75

Virtue, Tessa, 49

Waldo-Baltzer, Carolyn, 49
Watt-Cloutier, Sheila, 75
Wheeler, Anne, 32
White, Portia, 45
Wickenheiser, Hayley, 75
Wieland, Joyce, 50
Wieman, Cornelia, 21
Wilson, Alice, 75
Wilson, Barbara, 32
Wilson, Bertha, 38
Wilson, Cairine, 56, 57
Wilson, Stacy, 49

Yeats, Karen, 40

Zimmerman, Rachel, 34

*For Margaret Ann Riddell Paterson,
a great Canadian woman, deeply loved
and admired. Dedicated with affection
and appreciation from her family. — E.M.*

*To every Canadian girl who dreams of
doing great things — M.F.*

....

Acknowledgements

Many, many thanks to the wonderful Canadian women at Kids Can Press, especially editor Katie Scott and also Yvette Ghione, Naseem Hrab, Olga Kidisevic, Genie MacLeod and Kate Patrick. Thanks to illustrator Maïa Faddoul for bringing the women in this book to life and to designer Karen Powers for making the words and images look so great together. I'm also very grateful to Gail Cuthbert Brandt, Professor Emerita, Renison University College, and Tiffany Morris for reviewing this manuscript.

Special thanks to Alix McEwen, Reference Archivist, Library and Archives Canada. Many thanks to Nivatha Balendra, Michal Crawley, Denise Dwyer, Susan R. Eaton, Dr. Lisa Gieg, Anjali Katta, Eric Le Marec, Douglas MacLeod, Melissa Sariffodeen, Hayley Todesco and Allison VanNest for their assistance with this book. Thanks also to Margaret Paterson's family for supporting this book. Many thanks to my brothers, Douglas and John. And I'm always grateful to Paul, a great Canadian man, not just now and then but always!

Kids Can Press gratefully acknowledges the financial support of the Government of Ontario, through Ontario Creates; the Ontario Arts Council; the Canada Council for the Arts; and the Government of Canada for our publishing activity.

Published in Canada and the U.S. by Kids Can Press Ltd.
25 Dockside Drive, Toronto, ON M5A 0B5

Kids Can Press is a Corus Entertainment Inc. company
www.kidscanpress.com

The artwork in this book was rendered digitally.
The text is set in Andis and Shandon Slab.

Edited by Katie Scott
Designed by Karen Powers

Printed and bound in Shenzhen, China, in 10/2019
by C&C Offset

FSC
www.fsc.org
MIX
Paper from
responsible sources
FSC® C008047

CM 20 0 9 8 7 6 5 4 3 2 1

Library and Archives Canada Cataloguing in Publication

Title: Canadian women now and then : more than 100 stories of fearless trailblazers / written by Elizabeth MacLeod ; illustrated by Maïa Faddoul.

Names: MacLeod, Elizabeth, author. | Faddoul, Maïa, 1994– illustrator.

Description: Includes bibliographical references and index.

Identifiers: Canadiana 20190114495 | ISBN 9781525300615 (hardcover)

Subjects: LCSH: Women — Canada — Biography — Juvenile literature.

Classification: LCC FC26.W6 M328 2020 | DDC j920.720971 — dc23